American History

Building Fluency

through Practice and Performance

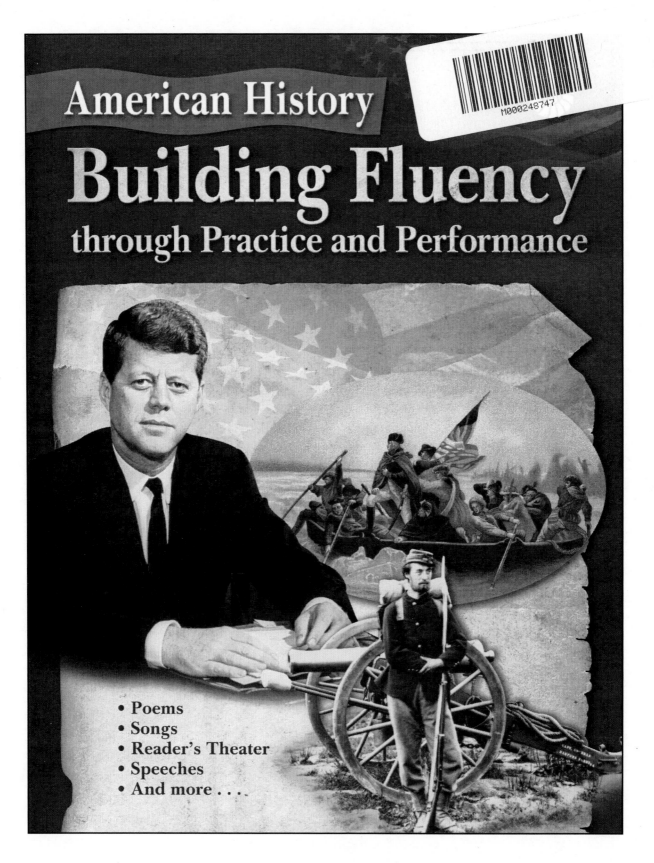

- Poems
- Songs
- Reader's Theater
- Speeches
- And more . . . .

Written and Compiled by

Timothy Rasinski and Lorraine Griffith

SHELL EDUCATION

Contributing Authors
Stephen Griffith
Wendy Conklin, M.A.

Assistant Editor
Torrey Maloof

Associate Editor
Christina Hill, M.A.

Editorial Assistant
Kathryn R. Kiley

Editorial Director
Emily R. Smith, M.A.Ed.

Editor-in-Chief
Sharon Coan, M.S.Ed.

Editorial Manager
Gisela Lee, M.A.

Creative Director
Lee Aucoin

Cover Designer
Neri Garcia

Cover Art
The Library of Congress
Victorian Traditions/Shutterstock, Inc.
Alfred Eisenstaedt/Time Life Pictures/
    Getty Images

Illustration Manager
Timothy J. Bradley

Imaging
Phil Garcia
Don Tran

Publisher
Corinne Burton, M.A.Ed.

Shell Education
5301 Oceanus Drive
Huntington Beach, CA 92649
http://www.shelleducation.com
ISBN 978-1-4258-0113-7
© *2007 by Shell Educational Publishing, Inc.*
Reprinted 2012

Table of Contents

Table of Contents *(cont.)*

Foreword

By Dr. Timothy Rasinski, Kent State University

We are so glad you have chosen this book, *Building Fluency through Practice and Performance*, which is a collection of reading texts of various genres related to America and American history. Whether you are an American history teacher, a reading teacher, or an English teacher, we think you will find this book invaluable in helping students revisit history through the voices of those who made the history. It will also help in developing proficient and fluent readers and a deeper understanding and appreciation for various genres of voice. We are primarily reading teachers interested in developing fluent and proficient readers. However, we are also teachers of American history and culture who see the reading of historical documents of various genres that embed a sense of author's voice as a way to make the history and English curriculum come alive for many students.

This book is a collection of poems, songs, scripts, documents, and other material related to various aspects of the American experience. Some of the material is original source; other material has been woven together by us and others to create texts that make the voice of history come alive again. Each selection, then, is a touchstone to one or more key characters or events that have shaped America as we know it today. We encourage you to use this book as a resource to make the study of American history come alive for students.

How you use this book is really up to you. We suggest that you select passages that are relevant to topics in American history that are currently under study or that are related to current events or dates. Assign selections to individuals or groups of students. Feel free to assign the same passage to more than one individual or group. Allow students to practice or rehearse the passages with a focus on reading the selection orally with appropriate expression and meaning. Be sure to not focus on reading the passage quickly. Fluency in reading has been defined by some as merely reading fast—this is an incorrect interpretation of fluency. We want to emphasize reading with expression and meaning—not speed. The rehearsal time can be one day to several days, depending on the complexity. While students rehearse, be sure to model expressive reading. Then, listen to their rehearsals and provide formative feedback and encouragement to students. Finally, arrange a time for students to perform their selections to the rest of the class or another audience.

The guided reading practice that is part of the rehearsal process is essential to students' reading development. Research has shown that guided rehearsals lead to substantial improvements in students' reading fluency and comprehension. Moreover, when the practice is done on authentic and meaningful materials and students are given opportunities to perform their selections for an enthusiastic audience, they will learn greater content, appreciate genres beyond narration (stories) and exposition (informational texts), and develop a sense of confidence in themselves as readers and learners that is essential to their ultimate success in school and life.

This book provides you with a way to make learning reading, English, and American history a win-win-win situation for your students and yourself. Have fun. Appreciate this wonderful language of ours—the language that patriots have used to make the case for this wonderful land of liberty!

Introduction to Teaching Fluency

Why This Book?

This book was developed in response to the need we have heard from teachers for good texts for teaching reading fluency within the content areas. Within the past several years, reading fluency has become recognized as an essential element in elementary and middle grade reading programs. Readers who are fluent are better able to comprehend what they read. They decode words so effortlessly that they can devote their cognitive resources to the all-important task of comprehension instead of bogging themselves down in decoding words they confront in their reading. They can also construct meaning (comprehension) by reading with appropriate expression and phrasing.

Readers develop fluency through guided practice and repeated readings—reading a text selection several times to the point where it can be expressed meaningfully—with appropriate expression and phrasing. Readers who engage in regular repeated readings, under the guidance and assistance of a teacher or other coach, improve their word recognition, reading rate, comprehension, and overall reading proficiency.

Students will find the texts in this book interesting and sometimes challenging. Students will especially want to practice the texts if you provide regular opportunities for them to perform the texts for their classmates, parents, or other audiences.

So, have fun with these passages. Read them with your students and read them again. Be assured that if you regularly have your students read and perform the texts in this book, you will go a long way to develop fluent readers who are able to decode words effortlessly and construct meaning through their interpretations of texts.

How to Use These Texts

The texts in this book are meant to be read, reread, and performed. If students do this, they will improve their ability to recognize words accurately and effortlessly and read with meaningful expression and phrasing. However, you, the teachers, are the most important part in developing instruction that uses these texts. In this section, we recommend ways to use the texts with your students.

Depending on the reading levels of your students, you may find some of these pieces too difficult to use at the beginning of the year. Instead, focus on the pieces that are rewritten or pieces where the original reading level is lower. Unfortunately for students today, we write differently now than the people of the past. What that means for our students is that they often have to decipher very difficult and complex writing just to read a primary source text from long ago. This book is set up to help your students be successful as they tackle writings from the past. Instead of just reading the text once and moving on, the students practice and reread the pieces in preparation for authentic presentations. That way, not only does their fluency grow through careful repetition, but as the class discusses the pieces, the students' comprehension improves as well.

Introduction to Teaching Fluency *(cont.)*

How to Use These Texts *(cont.)*

Types of Texts

There are basically four types of readings in this book: poems, reader's theater scripts, monologues, and songs. Some general suggestions for performing each are listed below:

- **Poems (and songs read orally):** These should be interpreted with meaning as the foremost guiding principle. Students should practice reading to the punctuation as opposed to reading line-by-line. If you choose to divide the selections into parts, they should be divided with close attention to meaningful phrases and thoughts rather than just by the layout of the text.

- **Reader's Theaters:** The scripts should be performed as written. A list of how many readers are needed is given at the top of each script. If the scripts are especially long, you may want to suggest more creative ways to perform the pieces. Otherwise, the audience may have trouble staying focused during the performance. Within the reader's theater scripts, any text taken from actual historic documents, speeches, letters, or quotations is italicized. Make sure you point this out to students as you introduce the pieces so they can see how the historic text has been interwoven with the rest of the script.

- **Monologues:** These pieces are to be performed by one speaker who is attempting to interpret the text for meaning in regard to the historical setting of the time. It is better not to break these pieces into multiple parts because they are meant for one voice.

- **Songs:** Most songs should be sung. They can be performed as choral readings, but having the students sing them is more meaningful, effective fluency practice. You could also choose to have students create rhythmic raps with percussion to go along with the songs.

Scheduling and Practice

The texts should be read repeatedly over several days. We recommend that you introduce one text at a time and practice it over the next three, four, or five days, depending on how quickly your students develop mastery over it. Write the text you are going to read on chart paper, copy it on an overhead transparency, or project the digital copy of the text. (Digital copies of the texts are provided on the Teacher Resource CD. Two digital versions of each text are provided. A PDF of each text can be projected for group reading or review of the texts. Copies of the texts are also provided in *Microsoft Word*™ files so that teachers can edit them as necessary for their students. See page 176 for more information.)

Have the students read the text several times each day. They should read it a couple times at the beginning of each day; read it several times during various breaks in the day; and read it multiple times at the end of each day.

Make two copies of the text for each student. Have students keep one copy in school in their "fluency folders." The other copy can be sent home for the students to continue practicing with their families. Communicate to families the importance of children continuing to practice the text at home with their parents and other family members.

How to Use These Texts *(cont.)*

Coaching Your Students

A key ingredient to repeated reading is the coaching that comes from a teacher. As your students practice reading the target text each week, alone, in small groups, or as an entire class, be sure to provide positive feedback about their reading. Help them develop a sense for reading the text in such a way that it conveys the meaning that the author attempts to convey or the meaning that the reader may wish to convey. Through oral interpretation of a text, readers can express joy, sadness, anger, surprise, or any of a variety of emotions. Help students learn to use their reading to convey this level of meaning.

Teachers do this by listening, from time to time, as students read and coaching them in the various aspects of oral interpretation. You may wish to suggest that students emphasize certain words, insert dramatic pauses, read a bit faster in one place, or slow down in other parts of the text. And, of course, lavish praise on students' best efforts to convey a sense of meaning through their reading. Although it may take a while for the students to learn to develop this sense of "voice" in their reading, in the long run, it will lead to more engaged and fluent reading and higher levels of comprehension.

Reader's Theater Scripts

Throughout the lessons in this book, you will find numerous reader's theater scripts. This is an exciting and easy method of providing students with the opportunity to practice fluency leading to a performance. Reader's theater minimizes the use of props, sets, costumes, and memorization. Students read from a book or prepared script using their fluent voices to bring text to life. Reader's theater has the following characteristics:

1. The script is always read and never memorized.

2. Readers may be characters or narrators, or they may switch back and forth.

3. The readers may sit, stand, or both, but they do not have to perform any other actions.

4. Readers use only eye contact, facial expressions, and vocal expression to express emotion.

5. Musical accompaniment or soundtracks may be used but are not necessary.

6. Very simple props may be used, especially with younger children, to help the audience identify the roles played by the readers.

7. Practice for the reader's theater should consist of coached repeated readings that lead to a smooth, fluent presentation.

Word Study

One goal of this book is to develop fluent and meaningful oral reading. A second goal is to increase student understanding of various historical periods from America's past. Comprehending and appreciating the vocabulary of the time periods is key to improving student understanding. Without knowledge of the language of the times, students cannot

How to Use These Texts *(cont.)*

Word Study *(cont.)*

fully comprehend or gain information from the texts. Practicing of passages provides opportunities to develop students' content-area vocabulary and word-decoding skills. Students may practice a passage repeatedly to the point where it is largely memorized. At this point, students may not look at the words in the text as closely as they should. By continually drawing attention to interesting and important words in the text, you can help students maintain their focus.

After reading a passage several times through, ask students to choose words from the passage that they think are interesting or historically important. Put these words on a word wall, or ask students to add them to their personal word banks. Talk about the words—their meanings and spellings. Brainstorm and list words that have similar meanings. Help students develop a deepened appreciation for these words. Encourage students to use these words in their oral and written language. You might, for example, ask students to use the chosen words in journal entries about the time period.

Once a list of words has been added to a classroom word wall or students' word banks, play various games with the words. Have students sort the chosen words along a variety of dimensions—by syllable, part of speech, historic context, or by meaning. Through sorting-and-categorizing activities, students get repeated exposure to words, examining the words differently with each sort.

No matter how you do it, make the opportunity to examine selected words from the passages part of your regular instructional routine for these fluency texts. The time spent in word study will most definitely improve students' overall fluency and comprehension.

Performance

One of the most important keys to improving fluency is that the students practice reading the pieces for authentic reasons. If the final presentations are always just to your class, students will quickly lose interest. Once they have lost interest in the performance, they will not work as hard at perfecting their fluency. You will not see as much growth in your students if they feel that all their practice is for nothing. Instead, be creative and have fun as you plan performance presentations.

Always allow several days of practice for each piece. Then, arrange a special time for the students to perform the text. This performance time can range from 5 minutes to 30 minutes. Find special people (such as the principal, music teacher, or media specialist) to listen to your children perform. You may also want to invite a neighboring class, parents, or another group (e.g., local government officials, military veterans, people from service organizations) to come to your room to listen to the performance. Classes with younger students make great audiences if the content is something they are also studying. Have the students perform the targeted text as a group. Later, you can have individuals or groups of children perform the text again as well as other texts that have been practiced previously.

Performance *(cont.)*

As an alternative to having your children perform for a group that comes to your room, you may want to send your children to visit other adults and students in the building. Principals, school secretaries, music teachers, art teachers, custodians, aides, and visitors to the building are usually great audiences for students' readings. Tape recording and videotaping your students is another way to create performance opportunities.

If you have a hard time finding people to whom your class can present, try to tie the presentations into celebrations or holidays. Or, make the presentations part of school-wide events. For example, you could have your students add to the school's morning announcements or perform the opening song for an assembly. Rather than holding your own assemblies, work with other teachers to hold Poetry Celebrations where students read historical poetry.

Regardless of how you do it, it is important that you create opportunities for your students to perform for different audiences. The magic of the performance will give students the motivation to want to practice their assigned texts. Your students' fluency will only improve if you make the performances important and authentic.

Concluding Thoughts

Dr. Rasinski has a website dedicated to helping teachers as they develop their students' fluency. The website lists information about Dr. Rasinski's schedule as well as books, websites, and other resources to support teachers. Visit **http://www.timrasinski.com**.

Remember that the key to developing fluency is guided oral and silent reading practice. Students become more fluent when they read the texts repeatedly. Reading requires students to actually see the words in the texts. Thus, it is important that you do not require students to memorize the texts they are practicing and performing. Memorization leads students away from visually examining the words. Although students may want to try to memorize some texts, the instructional emphasis needs to be on reading with expression so that any audience will enjoy the students' oral renderings of the texts. Keep students' eyes on the texts whenever possible.

One of the most important things we can do to promote proficient and fluent reading is to have students practice reading meaningful passages with a purpose: to perform them. This book provides students with opportunities to create meaning with their voices as well as the wonderful words in these primary sources and other historical texts.

America—
An Overview

I Hear America Singing

By Walt Whitman

I hear America singing, the varied carols I hear;

Those of mechanics—each one singing his, as it should be, blithe and strong;

The carpenter singing his, as he measures his plank or beam,

The mason singing his, as he makes ready for work, or leaves off work;

The boatman singing what belongs to him in his boat—the deckhand singing on the steamboat deck;

The shoemaker singing as he sits on his bench—the hatter singing as he stands;

The wood-cutter's song—the ploughboy's, on his way in the morning, or at the noon intermission, or at sundown;

The delicious singing of the mother—or of the young wife at work—or of the girl sewing or washing—Each singing what belongs to her, and to none else;

The day what belongs to the day—at night, the party of young fellows, robust, friendly,

Singing, with open mouths, their strong melodious songs.

Background Information

Walt Whitman is considered one of the greatest American poets. He wrote this poem after the Civil War when America began to move from being an agricultural country to a manufacturing nation. This poem appears in his book, *Leaves of Grass*.

Performance Suggestion

Practice and perform this poem with a group of classmates. Divide the poem up by the different occupations that Whitman hears. Discuss the feelings that Whitman is trying to portray through his words.

#50113—American History Texts for Fluency Practice © *Shell Education*

From the Mouths and Pens of the American Presidents

Written and Compiled by Lorraine Griffith

Directions

This is a reader's theater for a pair of students. Both students read the bold type. Then, one student reads the background information and the other student reads the quotation. Teams of two can rotate throughout the script, or divide the script into sections and have different pairs read the various parts.

George Washington 1789–1797

In 1789, George Washington became our nation's first president. As reflected in his inauguration day thoughts, he took very seriously that he would set the standard for the presidency.

> *"I must show by words and actions how free men resolve their fights. I must balance all the factions—calm the zealots for States' rights. I must set the first example of what a President should be, as I walk on untrodden ground with no path in place for me."*

John Adams 1797–1801

As our second president, John Adams, was more of a political thinker than a politician. He lived through the American Revolution and appreciated the cost of becoming a nation.

> *"People and nations are forged in the fires of adversity."*

Thomas Jefferson 1801–1809

In 1801, Thomas Jefferson became the third president of the United States. He will be forever remembered for writing the following words in the Declaration of Independence.

> *"We hold these truths to be self-evident, that all men are created equal, that they are endowed by their Creator with certain unalienable Rights, that among these are Life, Liberty and the pursuit of Happiness."*

From the Mouths and Pens of the American Presidents *(cont.)*

James Madison 1809–1817

Our fourth president, James Madison, was known as the Father of the Constitution. Madison understood the job to be a result of many men's ideas. He had great love for his new nation. After he died in 1836, someone opened a note from him and found this now-famous quotation.

> *"The advice nearest to my heart and deepest in my convictions is that the Union of the States be cherished and perpetuated."*

James Monroe 1817–1825

James Monroe was the fifth president. He presided during the "Era of Good Feelings." He was most famous for limiting European intervention in the affairs of the countries of the Western Hemisphere through his Monroe Doctrine.

> *". . . the American continents, by the free and independent condition which they have assumed and maintain, are henceforth not to be considered as subjects for future colonization by any European powers."*

John Quincy Adams 1825–1829

As our sixth president, John Quincy Adams was nicknamed "Old Man Eloquent." He was known for his way with words and depth of thought. He believed in looking at the challenges of a nation honestly and clearly.

> *"Facts are stubborn things; and whatever may be our wishes, our inclinations, or the dictates of our passions, they cannot alter the state of facts and evidence."*

Andrew Jackson 1829–1837

Our seventh president, Andrew Jackson, was nicknamed "Old Hickory." Born in the Carolina settlements, his perspective in leadership came from the view of a common citizen, not a privileged aristocrat.

> *"Every good citizen makes his country's honor his own, and cherishes it not only as precious but as sacred. He is willing to risk his life in its defense and is conscious that he gains protection while he gives it."*

From the Mouths and Pens of the American Presidents *(cont.)*

Martin Van Buren 1837–1841

Martin Van Buren, our eighth president, served the country during a difficult financial struggle that began just a few months after he took over the job. He is well known for wanting to do things carefully and correctly.

> *"It is easier to do a job right than to explain why you didn't."*

William Henry Harrison 1841

Our ninth president, William Henry Harrison, was only in office for a few months because he died of pneumonia. Although he was born into a wealthy family of Virginians, he spent much of his life in sparsely settled territories. He said this about government:

> *"I contend that the strongest of all governments is that which is most free."*

John Tyler 1841–1845

Nicknamed "His Accidency" by some, John Tyler came into office by default. The president had died, and he was sworn in because he was vice president. The way he came into office caused problems with his term as the tenth president. He reflects on this issue in the following quotation:

> *"If the tide of defamation and abuse shall turn, and my administration come to be praised, future vice presidents who may succeed to the presidency may feel some slight encouragement to pursue an independent course."*

James K. Polk 1845–1849

President James Polk added a vast area to the United States, but its acquisition precipitated a bitter quarrel between the North and the South over expansion of slavery. As the 11th president, he worked hard and felt the presidency was a total commitment of time and energy.

> *"No president who performs his duties faithfully and conscientiously can have any leisure."*

From the Mouths and Pens of the American Presidents *(cont.)*

Zachary Taylor 1849–1850

The 12th president, Zachary Taylor was a career military man who did not vote until age 62. Although he was a Southern slaveholder, "Old Rough and Ready" was determined to preserve the Union during a tense time in American history. He died after only 500 days in office.

> *"I have always done my duty. I am ready to die. My only regret is for the friends I leave behind me."*

Millard Fillmore 1850–1853

As states' rights became more of a divisive issue, the 13th president, Millard Fillmore, tried his best to create compromise between the North and the South. Although the Compromise of 1850 became law, it did not accomplish a long-lasting unity.

> *"May God save the country, for it is evident that the people will not."*

Franklin Pierce 1853–1857

Franklin Pierce was our 14th president. He backed the Kansas-Nebraska Act that permitted some new western territories to decide for themselves if slavery should be allowed in those areas. Some believe this act was the beginning of the Civil War.

> *"I wish I could indulge higher hope for the future of our country, but the aspect of any vision is fearfully dark and I cannot make it otherwise."*

James Buchanan 1857–1861

Our 15th president, James Buchanan, was still hopeful that compromise would keep the rapidly dividing nation together. He was gifted in debate and believed he could hold the nation together with proper interpretation of the constitutional law.

> *"I like the noise of democracy."*

From the Mouths and Pens of the American Presidents *(cont.)*

Abraham Lincoln 1861–1865

Our 16th president, Abraham Lincoln, is one of the most memorable presidents because of the dignity he maintained during such a tense time in United States history. The Civil War took the nation through an unprecedented time of peril but ended under his leadership. His words have been memorized by millions of elementary students since they were first spoken in the Gettysburg Address in 1863.

> *"Fourscore and seven years ago our fathers brought forth on this continent, a new nation, conceived in Liberty, and dedicated to the proposition that all men are created equal."*

Andrew Johnson 1865–1869

After President Lincoln died from an assassin's bullet, Vice President Andrew Johnson became the 17th president. He was given a huge task of beginning the healing process between the Union and the Confederate states. Although he was the first president to be impeached, he was a man of great courage while he served.

> *"Honest conviction is my courage; the Constitution is my guide."*

Ulysses S. Grant 1869–1877

Our 18th president, Ulysses S. Grant, was better known as a Union military general during the Civil War than as a president. His nickname, "Unconditional Surrender Grant," came from a battle in which he was asked by the Confederacy to give his terms for surrender. He said his most famous words.

> *"No terms except an unconditional and immediate surrender can be accepted."*

Rutherford B. Hayes 1877–1881

Rutherford B. Hayes was our 19th president. He waited four months after the election to find out that he was actually chosen as president. Because the election was so close, a compromise required that the remaining Union soldiers leave the South. The period known as the Reconstruction finally ended.

> *"Nothing brings out the lower traits of human nature like office-seeking. Men of good character and impulses are betrayed by it into all sorts of meanness."*

From the Mouths and Pens of the American Presidents *(cont.)*

James A. Garfield 1881

James Garfield was our 20th president, but he was only in office for six months due to an assassin's bullet. During his short time in office, he was known as a hardworking president who wanted to reform the government and politics. He was a man of strong character and the last of the "log-cabin presidents."

> *"I mean to make myself a man, and if I succeed in that, I shall succeed in everything else."*

Chester A. Arthur 1881–1885

It was said of our 21st president, "No man ever entered the Presidency so profoundly and widely distrusted, and no one ever retired . . . more generally respected." While in office, Chester Arthur began the Civil Service test. That meant certain government jobs could be received only through rigorous written examinations, not because of political favor.

> *"Since I came here, I have learned that Chester A. Arthur is one man and the President of the United States is another."*

Grover Cleveland 1885–1889 and 1893–1897

Our 22nd president, Grover Cleveland, was also the 24th president. He holds two distinctions, the only president to be counted twice and the only one to get married while serving in the White House. Although Cleveland worked hard to lower the surplus of money in the treasury and to clean up mismanaged funds in government, he failed.

> *"The ship of democracy, which has weathered all storms, may sink through the mutiny of those on board."*

Benjamin Harrison 1889–1893

Our 23rd president, Benjamin Harrison, was sandwiched between the two presidencies of Grover Cleveland. Harrison managed to expand the navy and steamship lines, tried to annex Hawaii as a state, and worked to lower the tariffs on imports.

> *"I pity the man who wants a coat so cheap that the man or woman who produces the cloth will starve in the process."*

From the Mouths and Pens of the American Presidents *(cont.)*

William McKinley 1897–1901

William McKinley, our 25th president, was peace loving but faced several hard international situations. As a result, he saw the Spanish-American War during his tenure as president, which ended with his own assassination.

"War should never be entered upon until every agency of peace has failed."

Theodore Roosevelt 1901–1909

Our 26th president, Theodore Roosevelt, was applauded for his progressive reforms at home, especially with conservation. His foreign policy was guided by the proverb, "Speak softly and carry a big stick." He also said,

"If you could kick the person in the pants responsible for most of your trouble, you wouldn't sit for a month."

William Howard Taft 1909–1913

William Howard Taft, our 27th president, had the difficult task of following the very popular Roosevelt. He was reluctant to be president but felt pressured to run. He later became the Chief Justice of the Supreme Court and was fulfilled in that job.

"Presidents come and go, but the Supreme Court goes on forever."

Woodrow Wilson 1913–1921

Woodrow Wilson was a brilliant teacher and college president before becoming our nation's 28th president. He led the U.S. military into World War I and promoted the League of Nations, which was like today's United Nations. He believed in democracy.

"The ear of the leader must ring with the voices of the people."

Warren G. Harding 1921–1923

Before our 29th president, Warren Harding, completed his term, he died of a heart attack. He helped reduce the workday from twelve hours a day to eight. However, his legacy is marked with scandal that surfaced after his death.

"I have no trouble with my enemies. I can take care of my enemies in a fight. But my friends, . . . they're the ones who keep me walking the floor at nights!"

From the Mouths and Pens of the American Presidents *(cont.)*

Calvin Coolidge 1923–1929

Our 30th president, Calvin Coolidge, was a quiet man. He was thrifty. He never owned a car and purchased his first house after leaving the presidency. Ironically, he was president during the Roaring Twenties and the Jazz Age, a time of prosperity. His quiet spirit led him to say,

> *"It takes a great man to be a good listener."*

Herbert Hoover 1929–1933

Our 31st president, Herbert Hoover, lost both of his parents by the age of nine. He worked hard, attended college, and became an engineer. He was known as a great humanitarian during World War I and served as president during the Great Depression.

> *"My country owes me nothing. It gave me, as it gives every boy and girl, a chance. It gave me schooling, independence of action, opportunity for service and honor. In no other land could a boy from a country village, without inheritance or influential friends, look forward with unbounded hope."*

Franklin D. Roosevelt 1933–1945

Franklin Delano Roosevelt, our 32nd president, was elected four times. In response to the Depression of the 1930s, he insured bank deposits and created the New Deal, which was an attempt to bring immediate relief to the needy and recovery to the economy. He was a strong leader for the country during World War II.

> *"First of all, let me assert my firm belief that the only thing we have to fear is fear itself—nameless, unreasoning, unjustified terror which paralyzes needed efforts to convert retreat into advance."*

Harry S. Truman 1945–1953

Our 33rd president was rushed into the presidency when Roosevelt died suddenly of a cerebral hemorrhage. Harry Truman had to make many decisions concerning the economy, the atomic bomb, and foreign affairs. He served two terms as president. He reflects in this quotation:

> *"In reading the lives of great men, I found that the first victory they won was over themselves . . . self-discipline with all of them came first."*

 #50113—Building Fluency through Practice and Performance

From the Mouths and Pens of the American Presidents *(cont.)*

Dwight D. Eisenhower 1953–1961

Dwight D. Eisenhower, the 34th president, was a victorious military general during World War II. He had a reputation for integrity of character. He worked to obtain an end to the fighting in the Korean War and assisted nations in developing atomic energy for peaceful uses.

> *"What counts is not necessarily the size of the dog in the fight—it's the size of the fight in the dog."*

John F. Kennedy 1961–1963

Our 35th president, John F. Kennedy, was called upon to handle a crisis in Cuba when it was learned that the Soviets had nuclear missiles there. He forever changed the Democratic Party through his concern for civil rights and his work to end segregation. His presidency ended with his assassination in Dallas, Texas.

> *"And so, my fellow Americans: ask not what your country can do for you—ask what you can do for your country. My fellow citizens of the world: ask not what America will do for you, but what together we can do for the freedom of man."*

Lyndon B. Johnson 1963–1969

Only 99 minutes after Kennedy's shocking assassination, Lyndon B. Johnson was sworn in as our 36th president. Although Johnson worked hard on domestic issues such as anti-poverty measures, Medicare, and civil rights, he is remembered most often for America's increased role in the Vietnam Conflict.

> *"America is not merely a nation but a nation of nations."*

Richard M. Nixon 1969–1974

Our 37th president, Richard M. Nixon, was successful in improving relations with China and the Soviet Union. He saw a cease-fire come to Vietnam through the Paris Peace Talks, and he spoke of peace. However, he will always be remembered for his involvement in the Watergate Scandal.

> *"The greatest honor history can bestow is that of peacemaker."*

From the Mouths and Pens of the American Presidents *(cont.)*

Gerald R. Ford 1974–1977

Gerald R. Ford, the 38th president, was the first to be in office through appointment. He was never elected by the people as vice president or president. The country was in economic recession and was reeling from Watergate. Ford is credited with helping to heal the wounds of our country.

> *"My fellow Americans, our long national nightmare is over."*

Jimmy Carter 1977–1981

Jimmy Carter, a Baptist peanut farmer from Georgia, was elected our 39th president. He worked to lessen the economic hardships at home, helped to encourage peace in the Middle East, and worked through his last day in office to bring the Iran hostages home safely. Since his presidency, he has continued his work in human rights through Habitat for Humanity.

> *"We become not a melting pot but a beautiful mosaic. Different people, different beliefs, different yearnings, different hopes, different dreams."*

Ronald Reagan 1981–1989

Ronald Reagan, our 40th president, was named "The Great Communicator" because of his memorable speeches. He made an effort to invigorate the economy and lessen America's dependency on government. Through five historic meetings with the head of the Soviet Union, he was able to finally see progress in the Cold War resolution.

> *"Mr. Gorbachev, tear down this wall!"*

George H. W. Bush 1989–1993

Our 41st president, George H. W. Bush, came into the presidency when everything was changing. The Soviet Union broke into smaller countries and events involving the drug trade in Panama were tense. He is most remembered for Desert Storm in Kuwait, which began with Saddam Hussein's invasion of that country.

> *"America is never wholly herself unless she is engaged in high moral principle. We as a people have such a purpose today. It is to make kinder the face of the nation and gentler the face of the world."*

#50113—Building Fluency through Practice and Performance

From the Mouths and Pens of the American Presidents *(cont.)*

William J. Clinton 1993–2001

William J. Clinton, our 42nd president, served two terms in office. Although scandal followed him throughout his presidency, he oversaw great domestic growth in the economy and had the first balanced budget in many years. His foreign involvement included work in the Middle East, the Balkans, Kosovo, and Russia.

> *"There is nothing wrong with America that cannot be cured by what is right with America."*

George W. Bush 2001–2009

Our 43rd president, George W. Bush, came into office after months of debate over the election results. As the nation was transformed by the events of September 11, 2001, his presidency became dominated by homeland security and the war against terrorism.

> *"Terrorist attacks can shake the foundations of our biggest buildings, but they cannot touch the foundation of America. These acts shatter steel, but they cannot dent the steel of American resolve."*

Barack Obama 2009–present

Our 44th president, Barack Obama, is the first African American president in United States history. His presidency began during an economic recession and the War in Iraq.

> *"Tonight, we gather to affirm the greatness of our nation—not because of the height of our skyscrapers, or the power of our military, or the size of our economy. Our pride is based on a very simple premise, summed up in a declaration made over two hundred years ago."*

> *ALL: "We hold these truths to be self-evident, that all men are created equal, that they are endowed by their Creator with certain unalienable rights, that among these are life, liberty, and the pursuit of happiness."*

Extension Suggestions

- Create a wax museum where you dress as the presidents. Each student would speak only when it was time for his or her president's quotation.

- Create a multimedia slide for each president. Each slide could include a famous portrait and one significant achievement as president. Students could record the quotations to play within the presentation.

November: A Time of Thanks and Remembrance in America in Poetry, Song, and Speech

By Timothy Rasinski

A reader's theater for four voices

R1: November is the time we give thanks in America.

R2: That's why we celebrate Thanksgiving on the fourth Thursday of November of every year. It helps us remember the first Thanksgiving—a celebration of American Indians and the Pilgrims from England.

R3: It was President Abraham Lincoln who proclaimed, in 1863, that the last Thursday in November be set aside as a day of thanks for all the blessings our country has received over the past year.

R4: In the middle of the bloody Civil War, Lincoln still found it appropriate to give thanks. He wrote:

R2: *"It has seemed to me fit and proper that these blessings should be solemnly, reverently and gratefully acknowledged, as with one heart and one voice, by the whole of the American people."*

R1: November 1863 also marked a journey taken by President Lincoln—a trip to Gettysburg, Pennsylvania.

R3: There he was asked to help dedicate a cemetery to the brave soldiers who had been killed in the Battle of Gettysburg earlier that year.

R4: He spoke about those courageous soldiers who had saved the country.

R1: But, he also reminded the living, those alive in 1863 and those of us living today, that there is much that we still need to do to keep the spirit of America alive.

#50113—Building Fluency through Practice and Performance   © *Shell Education*

November: A Time of Thanks and Remembrance in America in Poetry, Song, and Speech *(cont.)*

R2: *"It is for us the living, rather, to be dedicated here to the unfinished work which they who fought here have thus far so nobly advanced. It is rather for us to be here dedicated to the great task remaining before us—*

R3: *that from these honored dead we take increased devotion to that cause for which they gave the last full measure of devotion—that we here highly resolve that these dead shall not have died in vain—that this nation, under God, shall have a new birth of freedom—and that*

All: ***government of the people, by the people, for the people,***

R1: *shall not perish from the earth."*

R4: Less than 60 years later, America was engaged in another war—the First World War.

R3: It was the war that President Woodrow Wilson hoped would, *"Make the world safe for democracy."*

R2: That war ended on November 11, 1918—on the eleventh hour of the eleventh day of the eleventh month. It was called Armistice Day.

R1: An *armistice* is a truce between armies or a time in which armies agree to stop fighting.

R3: But, as with all wars, soldiers die, and many American soldiers, sailors, and marines died during the First World War.

R4: So, Armistice Day became another November holiday where Americans remembered and gave thanks for those who died in service to their country.

R2: A famous poem was written during the First World War. It was written by a soldier named John McCrae who was thinking about all the soldiers who had been killed. They had fought for democracy and freedom.

November: A Time of Thanks and Remembrance in America in Poetry, Song, and Speech *(cont.)*

R4: This soldier was looking at a cemetery for soldiers in Flanders, Belgium, when he wrote his poem, "In Flanders Fields."

R1: *In Flanders fields the poppies blow*
Between the crosses, row on row

R2: *That mark our place; and in the sky*
The larks, still bravely singing, fly
Scarce heard amid the guns below.

R1: *We are the Dead.*
Short days ago we lived, felt dawn, saw sunset glow,

R2: *Loved and were loved,*
and now we lie in Flanders fields.

R3: *Take up our quarrel with the foe*
To you from failing hands we throw

R4: *The torch; be yours to hold it high.*
If you break faith with us who die

All: ***We shall not sleep, though poppies grow***
In Flanders fields.

R1: Children all around the United States and Canada recite "In Flanders Fields" every November 11.

R3: In the United States, we now call November 11 Veterans Day—a day to give thanks for veterans, those who served our country in the military services.

R2: In Canada, November 11 is called Remembrance Day.

November: A Time of Thanks and Remembrance in America in Poetry, Song, and Speech *(cont.)*

R4: By November 1938, America was on the verge of yet another war—the Second World War.

R3: Irving Berlin, a famous songwriter who had immigrated to America from Russia, wrote a song he hoped would inspire Americans as the world headed toward war again.

R2: And so, on November 11, 1938, the day set aside to give thanks and remember America's servicemen and women, Kate Smith, a renowned singer, sang Berlin's song on the radio for the first time—

R4: It was called "God Bless America."

R1: *While the storm clouds gather far across the sea,*

R2: *Let us swear allegiance to a land that's free,*

R3: *Let us all be grateful for a land so fair,*

R4: *As we raise our voices in a solemn prayer.*

All: **God Bless America,**
Land that I love.
Stand beside her, and guide her
Through the night with a light from above.
From the mountains, to the prairies,
To the oceans, white with foam
God bless America, My home sweet home.
God bless America, My home sweet home.

> ## Extension Suggestion
>
> Work in three different groups: Lincoln's Gettysburg Address, "In Flanders Fields," and "God Bless America." Rewrite the speech, poem, or song in your own words. After practicing, perform the new speech, poem, or song aloud.

The Promise of America

#50113—*Building Fluency through Practice and Performance* © *Shell Education*

Patriots, Tories, and Neutrals: Revolutionary Opinions

By Mrs. Griffith's Fifth Grade Class, 2005–2006
A choral reading for three groups of students

Patriots: We want independence!

Tories: We want loyalty to the king!

Neutrals: Whatever . . .

Patriots: Let's go to war!

Tories: Let's not!

Neutrals: Whatever . . .

Patriots: Bring it on!

Tories: Stay where you are!

Neutrals: We don't care! Whatever . . .

Patriots: Death to King George!

Tories: Long live the king!

Neutrals: Whatever . . .

Patriots: Freedom, Freedom!

Tories: Loyalty, Loyalty!

Neutrals: Loyalty, Shmoyalty, Freedom, Shmeedom! Whatever . . .

Patriots, Tories, and Neutrals: Revolutionary Opinions *(cont.)*

Patriots: Whatever the cost!

Tories: It costs too much!

Neutrals: Who cares! Whatever . . .

Patriots: War!

Tories: Peace!

Neutrals: What's for supper? Whatever . . .

Background Information

Not everyone in the colonies was ready to fight in the Revolutionary War. Some were Tories, which means they wanted to stay loyal to Great Britain and the king. Others were Patriots. They wanted to fight. The neutral people were not sure how they felt.

Extension Suggestion

Fifth graders who were studying the causes of the American Revolution wrote this piece. Their teacher suggested they think of things they would say based on their points of view. They brainstormed and the class wrote this piece during class. After some revising and editing, they enjoyed performing it over and over again. Now it is your turn. After performing this piece, work with your classmates to write and perform your own piece about the opinions before the American Revolution.

#50113—Building Fluency through Practice and Performance

© *Shell Education*

The Declaration of Independence

Adapted by Timothy Rasinski

A reader's theater for six voices: three narrators (N) and three readers of the Declaration of Independence (D)

N1: This is the story

N2: of the birth of the

N1–N3: United States of America.

N2: At one time the United States was made up of colonies of Great Britain. However, people in the colonies began to feel that the king of Great Britain was exerting more control over them than they felt was warranted.

N2–N3: Colonists began to call for the separation of the North American colonies from Great Britain. They began to call for independence.

N3: The king had imposed on the colonies laws and taxes that the colonists felt were unfair.

N1–N3: The king had also ignored petitions, or requests, from the colonies that their grievances be heard.

N1: And so, one by one, the various colonies began to demand independence from Great Britain. By May 1776, eight colonies had decided that they would support independence.

N2: On May 15, 1776, the largest colony, Virginia, resolved that:

N2–N3: *"The delegates appointed to represent this colony in General Congress be instructed to propose to that respectable body to declare the United Colonies free and independent states."*

N3: The Continental Congress was the governing body of the 13 colonies. It met a few weeks later in Philadelphia. On June 7, Richard Henry Lee of Virginia read this resolution to the Continental Congress:

The Declaration of Independence *(cont.)*

N1: *"Be it resolved: That these United Colonies are, and of right ought to be, free and independent States, that they are absolved from all allegiance to the British Crown, and that all political connection between them and the State of Great Britain is, and ought to be, totally dissolved."*

N2: A committee of five members was then formed to create a written statement of freedom from Great Britain.

N3: The members of the committee consisted of two men from New England: John Adams from Massachusetts and Roger Sherman from Connecticut;

N1: Two representatives from the middle colonies: Robert Livingston of New York and Benjamin Franklin from Pennsylvania;

N2: And one southerner: Thomas Jefferson from Virginia.

N3: Jefferson was given the primary task of writing the document.

N1: By the end of June, Jefferson had completed his declaration. It was sent to the Continental Congress on July 1.

N2: There was some discussion and revision to the declaration.

N3: And, although the independence that the colonies sought was not totally realized until several years later,

N1: the declaration began a new country whose history is still being written today—our country,

N1–N3: The United States of America.

N2: On July 4, 1776, the declaration was adopted by the Continental Congress. Church bells throughout Philadelphia rang out in celebration as the declaration was read to the people.

The Declaration of Independence *(cont.)*

D1–D3: *In Congress, July 4, 1776, the unanimous declaration of the 13 United States of America:*

D2: (slowly and deliberately) *When in the course of human events, it becomes necessary for one people to dissolve the political bands which have connected them with another, and to assume among the powers of the earth, the separate and equal station to which the Laws of Nature and of Nature's God entitle them,*

D3: *a decent respect to the opinions of mankind requires that they should declare the causes which impel them to the separation.*

D1: *We hold these truths to be self-evident, that all men are created equal, that they are endowed by their Creator with certain unalienable Rights*

All: ***That among these are Life, Liberty, and the pursuit of Happiness.***

D2: *That to secure these rights, Governments are instituted among Men, deriving their just powers from the consent of the governed.*

D1: *That whenever any Form of Government becomes destructive of these ends, it is the Right of the People to alter or abolish it and institute a new Government, laying its foundation on principles and organizing itself in a way that to them shall seem most likely to bring their Safety and Happiness.*

D3: *Prudence, indeed, will dictate that long established governments should not be changed for light and transient causes;*

D2: *But, when a long train of abuses reduces and oppresses the people, it is their right, it is their duty, to throw off such Government, and provide a new government for their future security.*

D1: *Such has been how the Colonies have suffered.*

D2: *And such is now the necessity which forces them to alter their former government.*

The Declaration of Independence *(cont.)*

D3: *The history of the present King of Great Britain is a history of repeated injuries and taking of rights and liberties, all done to establish an absolute Tyranny over these States . . . .*

D1: *In every stage of these Oppressions, we have petitioned for redress in the most humble terms from the King.*

D2: *Our repeated petitions have been answered only by repeated injury.*

D3: *A Prince whose character is thus marked by acts that define a Tyrant, is unfit to be the ruler of a free people . . . .*

D1: *We, therefore, the Representatives of the United States of America, in General Congress, assembled here,*

D2: *Appealing to the Supreme Judge of the world, do, in the Name, and by Authority of the good People of these Colonies, solemnly publish and declare*

D3: *That these United Colonies are, and of Right ought to be Free and Independent States,*

D2: *That they are absolved from all Allegiance to the British Crown,*

D1: *And that all political connection between them and the State of Great Britain, is and ought to be totally dissolved.*

D3: *And that as Free and Independent States, they have full Power to levy War, conclude Peace, contract Alliances, establish Commerce, and to do all other Acts and Things which Independent States may of right do.*

D1: *And for the support of this Declaration, with a firm reliance on the protection of divine Providence, we mutually pledge to each other our Lives, our Fortunes, and our sacred Honor.*

#50113—Building Fluency through Practice and Performance © *Shell Education*

The Declaration of Independence *(cont.)*

All: This is the story of the birth of the United States of America—
Our Country.

My country, 'tis of thee,
Sweet land of liberty,
Of thee I sing;
Land where my fathers died,
Land of the pilgrims' pride,
From every mountainside,
Let freedom ring!

Background Information

It took Jefferson about two weeks to write the Declaration of Independence. He borrowed his ideas of independence from an Englishman named John Locke who had lived years before. Up to that point, powerful rulers ran all nations. So, to declare independence was a very bold statement.

Extension Suggestion

Think about how King George III felt when he read these words. What would he have written in response to this document? Work with two friends to write a response. It should be a reader's theater for three voices. Then practice reading your response aloud. When you are ready, perform your piece for the rest of your class.

E PLURIBUS UNUM

By Lorraine Griffith
A reader's theater for three voices

R1: *E Pluribus Unum* (EE PLUR-uh-buhs YOO-nuhm)

R2: Out

R3: of

R1: many,

All: **One**

R1: Benjamin Franklin

R2: John Adams

R3: Thomas Jefferson

All: **Members of the first committee for the selection of the seal**

R1: 1776

R2: The motto appears on one side of every U.S. coin that is minted.

All: **Creation of one nation,**

R3: Out of 13

R2: different

R1: colonies

R2: Massachusetts

R3: New Hampshire

R1: Rhode Island

R2: Connecticut

R3: New York

R2: Pennsylvania

E PLURIBUS UNUM *(cont.)*

R1: New Jersey

R3: Delaware

R2: Maryland

R1: Virginia

R2: North Carolina

R3: South Carolina

R1: Georgia

All: **Join or Die! National unity**

R1: The Right

R2: of individual

R3: difference

All: *E Pluribus Unum*

R1: Out

R2: of

R3: many,

All: **One**

Performance Suggestion

Perform this with three individual students, three groups of students, or the whole class can be divided into three groups. Each group can take a different part: R1, R2, or R3. As you rehearse this script, be sure to say the words clearly and distinctly so that the audience can hear and fully appreciate the powerful words in this script.

Background Information

In 1776, a congressional committee was placed in charge of designing the seal of the United States. While working on this design, they suggested using *E PLURIBUS UNUM* as their new nation's motto. Their specific seal design was not chosen, but the motto was approved.

Preamble to the Constitution

By Lorraine Griffith; Adapted by Timothy Rasinski

A choral reading for a large group or a reader's theater for seven voices

R1:   The Constitution

R2:   of the United States of America.

All: *We the people*

R1:   The people:

R2:   First the American Indian,

R3:   then a flood of European immigrants,

R4:   Africans,

R5:   Middle Easterners,

R6:   Asian peoples,

R7:   South Americans

R1–R4:   And they keep on coming.

All: *We the people of the United States,*

R1:   The United States:

R2:   All 50!

R3:   From Portland, Maine, west to San Diego, California,

R4:   from Fargo, North Dakota, south to El Paso, Texas,

R5:   Alaska and Hawaii

Preamble to the Constitution *(cont.)*

All: *We the people of the United States, in order to form a more perfect Union,*

R6: That Union seemed perfect, all of the colonies became states as well as the territories to the west,

R7: until the southern states seceded because they wanted states' rights.

R1: But the Civil War ended with a more perfect union of states based upon the belief that all Americans deserved the right to life, liberty, and the pursuit of happiness.

All: *We the people of the United States, in order to form a more perfect Union, establish justice,*

R2: Even before the established United States, justice was valued.

R3: John Adams had actually defended the British in court after they had attacked and killed colonists during the Boston Massacre. Although he didn't believe in the British cause, he still believed justice was more important than retribution.

R4: Justice was ensured for Americans by following the fairness of John Adams in establishing a court system beginning with local courthouses and moving up to the Supreme Court in Washington, D.C.

All: *We the people of the United States, in order to form a more perfect Union, establish justice, insure domestic tranquility,*

R5: There have been times when our nation's tranquility has been disturbed.

R6: But in spite of Pearl Harbor, December 7, 1941,

R7: and the horror in New York City, Washington, D.C., and Pennsylvania, on September 11, 2001,

All: we still live in a stable and peaceful country.

Preamble to the Constitution *(cont.)*

All: *We the people of the United States, in order to form a more perfect Union, establish justice, insure domestic tranquility, provide for the common defense,*

R2: The Air Force. No one comes close! Soar to new heights in the wild blue yonder!

All: **Nothing can stop the U.S. Air Force!**

R3: The Army. Be all you can be! Be an army of one!

All: **Hoo Ahh!**

R4: The Navy, Welcome aboard;

All: **Anchors aweigh! Full speed ahead!**

R1: The Coast Guard, Protecting America. It's our job every day!

All: **Semper Paratus. Always Ready.**

R5: And the Marines. The few, the proud.

All: **Semper Fi!**

   We the people of the United States, in order to form a more perfect Union, establish justice, insure domestic tranquility, provide for the common defense, promote the general welfare,

R7: People's basic needs must be met in a country.

R5: Needs for housing, education, transportation, and health care are overseen by our government system.

R6: Labor laws ensure that people work in safe environments and that they are paid fairly for the work that they do.

Preamble to the Constitution *(cont.)*

All: *We the people of the United States, in order to form a more perfect Union, establish justice, insure domestic tranquility, provide for the common defense, promote the general welfare, and secure the blessings of liberty to ourselves*

R1: Jefferson's promise of Life, Liberty, and the Pursuit of happiness came later for many of the peoples of our nation.

R2: African Americans did not share the rights of whites by law until the Fourteenth Amendment in 1868.

R3: Women did not share in the rights of men to vote or own property until 1920 when the Suffrage Act was ratified.

R4: But people all around the world still look to the United States as the land of liberty for all.

All: *We the people of the United States, in order to form a more perfect Union, establish justice, insure domestic tranquility, provide for the common defense, promote the general welfare, and secure the blessings of liberty to ourselves and our posterity,*

R1: That's you and me!

R2–R3: And our children!

R4–R5: And our children's children.

R6–R7: And their children, too!

All: *We the people of the United States, in order to form a more perfect Union, establish justice, insure domestic tranquility, provide for the common defense, promote the general welfare, and secure the blessings of liberty to ourselves and our posterity, do ordain and establish this Constitution for the United States of America.*

Preamble to the Constitution *(cont.)*

R5: The Constitution of the United States of America has stood the test of time.

R6: Although it was signed on September 17, 1787, it still stands as a ruling document of laws, ensuring the rights and liberties that we still enjoy today.

R7: And so, let us proclaim once again for all the world to hear . . .

R1: The Preamble to the Constitution of the United States of America.

R2–R3: *We the people of the United States,*

R2–R5: *in order to form a more perfect Union,*

R2–R6: *establish justice, insure domestic tranquility,*

R2–R7: *provide for the common defense, promote the general welfare,*

All: **and secure the blessings of liberty, to ourselves and our posterity, do ordain and establish this Constitution for the United States of America.**

Background Information

The Preamble to the Constitution is one sentence that introduces the Constitution of the United States. The Preamble does not list any specific rights or powers. It just gives the reasons for writing the Constitution. It is believed that Gouverneur Morris, a founding father, wrote the Preamble to the Constitution.

Francis Scott Key's
"The Star-Spangled Banner"

By Lorraine Griffith

A reader's theater for six voices

R1:   Although we are all familiar with the tune and the first verse of the national anthem that is played at sporting events,

R2:   few people know the real truth behind the song.

R3:   The song is actually a story,

R4:   like a snapshot of a tense moment in United States history.

R5:   It was during the War of 1812,

R6:   a war between the young Americans and the British.

R1:   The conflict had been nasty, with the British burning both the Capitol and the White House in Washington, D.C.

R2:   It was now September 12, 1814,

R3:   two years into the war,

R4:   and two American men, Colonel John Skinner and Francis Scott Key, were visiting a British ship near Ft. McHenry, Maryland.

R5:   They were successful in releasing their friend, Dr. William Beanes,

R6:   who had been captured during the attack on Washington.

R1:   But before they were able to leave the ship,

R2–R3:   a battle ensued between the British and the Americans over Fort McHenry.

R4–R5:   These three American men were stuck on an enemy British ship watching the bombing of their own fort.

Francis Scott Key's
"The Star-Spangled Banner" *(cont.)*

R6: They watched through the nights of the 12th and 13th,
knowing that the British were well known for their victories at sea.

R1: *(quietly)* In the darkness of the 13th,

R2–R3: *(whisper)* the shelling stopped.

R4: *(hushed)* But the Americans on board the British ship could not see if the American flag was still flying above the fort.

R5: *(continued hush)* Was the battle victorious for the British or the Americans?

R6: *(with anticipation)* Francis Scott Key watched intently as the sun slowly rose

R1–R3: *(excitedly!)* and he was able to see the 42-foot long flag with its

R4: eight red stripes,

R5: seven white stripes,

R6: and 15 white stars waving proudly over Fort McHenry.

R1: He was moved to write on the back of an envelope the words to a poem he called "Defense of Fort McHenry."

R2: It was later that the words were put with a British drinking song tune

R3: and "The Star-Spangled Banner" was born.

R4: On March 3, 1931, this song was officially adopted as the national anthem of the United States of America.

Francis Scott Key's
"The Star-Spangled Banner" *(cont.)*

R5–R6:   Listen now to the words of our national anthem read as a poem.

R1:   Imagine you are on the deck of that enemy British ship,

R2–R3:   in the early dawn hours after the end of a vicious battle at sea,

R4:   wondering if you are on the winning side

R5:   or the losing . . . .

R6:   Watching for your flag,

All: **the symbol of victory . . . THE STAR-SPANGLED BANNER**

(As you read these familiar words, make every effort to create the wonder and anticipation of seeing the flag with your voice inflection.)

R1:   *Oh say,*

R2:   *can you see,*

R3:   *by the dawn's early light,*

R4:   *What so proudly we hail'd at the twilight's last gleaming?*

R5:   *Whose broad stripes and bright stars,*

R6:   *thro' the perilous fight,*

R3:   *O'er the ramparts we watch'd,*

R4:   *were so gallantly streaming?*

R5:   *And the rockets' red glare,*

R6:   *the bombs bursting in air,*

R3:   *Gave proof thro' the night that our flag was still there.*

Francis Scott Key's
"The Star-Spangled Banner" *(cont.)*

R1:   *O say,*

R2:   *does that star-spangled banner yet wave*
O'er the land of the free and the home of the brave?

R3:   *On the shore dimly seen thro' the mists of the deep,*

R4:   *Where the foe's haughty host in dread silence reposes,*

R5:   *What is that which the breeze,*

R6:   *o'er the towering steep,*

R5:   *As it fitfully blows,*

R2:   *half conceals,*

R1:   *half discloses?*

R1–R2: *Now it catches the gleam of the morning's first beam,*

R1–R4: *In full glory reflected,*

R1–R5: *now shines on the stream,*

All: ***'TIS THE STAR-SPANGLED BANNER***
O, long may it wave
O'er the land of the free and the home of the brave!

R1:   *And where is that band who so vauntingly swore*
That the havoc of war and the battle's confusion
A home and a country should leave us no more?

R2:   *Their blood has wash'd out their foul footsteps' pollution.*

Francis Scott Key's
"The Star-Spangled Banner" *(cont.)*

R3: *No refuge could save the hireling and slave*
From the terror of flight or the gloom of the grave:

All: **And the star-spangled banner in triumph doth wave**
O'er the land of the free and the home of the brave.

R4: *O thus be it ever when freemen shall stand,*
Between their lov'd home and the war's desolation;

R5: *Blest with vict'ry and peace,*

R6: *may the heav'n-rescued land*
Praise the Pow'r that hath made and preserv'd us a nation!

R1–R2: *Then conquer we must,*

R3–R4: *when our cause it is just,*

R5–R6: *And this be our motto:*

R1–R4: *"In God is our trust!"*

All: **And the star-spangled banner in triumph shall wave**
O'er the land of the free and the home of the brave!

Background Information

Francis Scott Key wrote a poem after watching British bombs land on Ft. McHenry during the War of 1812. Later, the words were sung to an old British tune. On March 3, 1931, Congress adopted the song, "The Star-Spangled Banner," as the national anthem of the United States of America.

My Name Is Old Glory

By Howard Schnauber; Arranged by Lorraine Griffith
A reader's theater for four readers

All: **I am the flag of the United States of America.**

R1:   My name is Old Glory.

R2:   I fly atop tall buildings.

R3:   I stand watch in America's halls of justice.

R4:   I fly majestically over great institutes of learning.

R1:   I stand guard with the greatest military power in the world.

All: **Look up!**

R2:   And see me!

R3:   I stand for peace—

R4:   honor—

R1:   truth

R2:   and justice.

R3:   I stand for freedom

R4:   I am confident—

R1–R2: I am arrogant

R3–R4: I am proud.

My Name Is Old Glory *(cont.)*

R1: When I am flown with my fellow banners

R2: My head is a little higher

R3: My colors a little truer.

All: **I bow to no one.**

R4: I am recognized all over the world.

R3: I am worshipped—

R2: I am saluted—

R1: I am respected

R2: I am revered—

R3: I am loved,

R4: and I am feared.

All: **I have fought every battle of every war for more than 200 years:**

R1: Gettysburg,

R2: Shiloh,

R3: Appomattox Court House,

R4: San Juan Hill,

R3: the trenches of France,

R2: the Argonne Forest,

R1: Anzio,

R2: Rome,

R3: the beaches of Normandy,

My Name Is Old Glory *(cont.)*

R4: the deserts of Africa, the cane fields of the Philippines,

R1: the rice paddies and jungles of Guam,

R2: Okinawa, Japan, Korea,

R3: Vietnam, Guadalcanal, New Britain,

R4: Peleliu, and many more islands.

R1: And a score of places long forgotten by all but those who were with me.

All: **I was there.**

R2: I led my soldiers—

R3: I followed them.

R4: I watched over them.

All: **They loved me.**

R1: I was on a small hill in Iwo Jima.

R2: I was dirty, battle-worn and tired, but my soldiers cheered me, and I was proud.

R3: I have been soiled, burned, torn, and trampled on in the streets of countries I have helped set free.

R4: It does not hurt,

All: **for I am invincible.**

R1: I have even been soiled,

My Name Is Old Glory *(cont.)*

R2:   burned,

R3:   torn,

R4:   and trampled on in the streets of my country,

R1:   but I shall overcome—

All: **for I am strong.**

R2:   I have slipped the bonds of Earth and stand watch over the uncharted new frontiers of space from my vantage point on the moon.

R3:   I have been a silent witness to all of America's finest hours.

R4:   But my finest hour comes when I am torn into strips to be used for bandages for my wounded comrades on the field of battle,

R2:   When I fly at half-mast to honor my soldiers,

R1:   And when I lie in the trembling arms of a grieving mother at the graveside of her fallen son.

All: **I am proud.**

R3:   My name is Old Glory.

All: **Long may I wave.**

Performance Suggestion

After reading through this piece, think about your voice and tone as you read through it again. Show emotion in your voice since this is a very emotional piece. Practice reading through the piece several times, adding vocal expression as you read.

Background Information

In 1831, a sea captain named William Driver exclaimed, "Old Glory!" when he saw his flag open up in the breeze at sea. And, that is where the name Old Glory came from.

© 1994 Mr. Howard Schnauber (Fort Collins Public Library Local History Archive, Oral History Interview of Mr. Howard Schnauber, the author)

The Statue of Liberty

By Lorraine Griffith

A reader's theater for three readers

All: **The Statue of Liberty**

R1: A gift from the people of France

R2: Over 100 years ago

R3: To the people of the United States

R1: As a symbol of friendship established during the American Revolution over 200 years ago.

R2: Now a symbol of freedom

R3: Democracy

R2: International friendship

All: **Welcome**

R1: To the United States of America

R2: Over 300 feet from ground to tip of torch

R3: An index finger eight feet long

R1: One eye, two-and-one-half feet across

R2: Thirty-one tons of copper

R3: One hundred twenty-five tons of steel

R1: Twenty-seven thousand tons of concrete

The Statue of Liberty *(cont.)*

R2:   Three hundred fifty-four steps from ground to crown

R3:   Twenty-two stories high

R1:   Twenty-five windows in the crown

R2:   Symbolizing natural minerals found on Earth

R3:   And heaven's rays shining over the world

R1:   A toga

R2:   The Ancient Republic of Rome

R3:   Torch

R1:   Enlightenment

R2:   Chains underfoot

All: **Liberty crushing the chains of slavery**

R3:   Seven rays of the Statue's crown

R2:   The seven seas

R1:   The seven continents

R1:   And on the tablet

R2:   In Roman numerals

All: **July 4, 1776**

R3:   America's Independence Day

The Statue of Liberty *(cont.)*

R1: President Grover Cleveland

R2: October 28, 1886

R3: Accepting the statue from France

All: **"We will not forget that Liberty has here made her home; nor shall her chosen altar be neglected."**

Background Information

The United States needed France's help to win the Revolutionary War against the British. With the help of Benjamin Franklin, both nations developed a friendship. In 1886, France gave the Statue of Liberty to the United States as a gift of that friendship. The huge statue was broken down into 350 pieces and shipped in 214 crates. Due to bad storms, the ship nearly sank at sea. Once at its destination, it took four months to reassemble.

Emma Lazarus and "The New Colossus"

By Lorraine Griffith
A reader's theater for two readers

R1: Emma Lazarus was an American poet born into a Jewish family on July 22, 1849.

R2: She was in her teens when she began writing poems.

R1: Miss Lazarus shared her poems with Ralph Waldo Emerson, an already famous American poet. But when he created a collection of poetry, her poems were conspicuously left out. She was not credited with greatness in her lifetime because she was a woman.

R2: And because she was Jewish, she knew what it was like to also be judged for her ethnicity. During the 1880s, there was a vicious wave of anti-Semitism sweeping through Eastern Europe. As these Jews found refuge in America, Lazarus became a speaker for her people.

R1: When the opportunity came in 1883 to help raise funds for a pedestal to hold the French-given Statue of Liberty, Emma Lazarus wrote a sonnet entitled "The New Colossus."

R2: A *colossus* is defined as a "statue that is several times larger than life size." In her sonnet, she transformed the "brazen giant" into a "Mother of Exiles."

R1: Her poem speaks to the heart of immigration from personal experience. She had comforted the "huddled masses yearning to live free" when she helped to welcome the Jews fleeing the Russian persecution.

R2: Since Emma Lazarus died at the young age of 38, she did not live to see her poem placed on a plaque at the base of the Statue of Liberty.

R1: A Jewish woman's words welcomed all newly immigrating Americans as they visited the "Mother of Exiles" in New York City.

Emma Lazarus and "The New Colossus" *(cont.)*

Both: "The New Colossus," by Emma Lazarus

R1: *Not like the brazen giant of Greek fame,*
with conquering limbs astride from land to land;

R2: *Here at our sea-washed, sunset gates*
shall stand a mighty woman with a torch,
whose flame is the imprisoned lightning,

R2: *and her name*

R1: *Mother of Exiles.*

R2: *From her beacon-hand glows world-wide welcome;*

R1: *her mild eyes command the air-bridged harbor that twin cities frame.*

Both: ***"Keep ancient lands, your storied pomp!"***

R2: *cries she with silent lips.*

Both: ***"Give me your tired, your poor, your huddled masses yearning to breathe free, the wretched refuse of your teeming shore. Send these, the homeless, tempest-tost to me, I lift my lamp beside the golden door!"***

Background Information

The first two lines of "The New Colossus" talk about a Greek statue called the Colossus of Rhodes. This statue is no longer standing today, but people who saw it long ago described it. The statue was the Greek god Helios and it was erected on the Greek island of Rhodes. It was about the same size as the Statue of Liberty.

★★★★★
★★★★
★★★
★

America's
Civil War

Events in the History of James W. C. Pennington: Formerly a Slave

Edited by Stephen Griffith; Arranged by Lorraine Griffith
A reader's theater for three voices

James: I was born a slave in the state of Maryland. In the spring of 1828, when I was 21, my master had me undertake the carpentering business. I had been working at this trade six days when I fled.

My master was greatly irritated and had resolved to have, as he said, "a general whipping-match among [the slaves because of tardiness]." He had a rope in his pocket, and a cowhide in his hand, walking about the premises, and speaking to every one he met in a very insolent manner, and finding fault with some without just cause. My father, among other numerous and responsible duties, discharged that of shepherd to a large and valuable flock of Merino sheep. This morning he was engaged in the tenderest of a shepherd's duties—a little lamb, not able to go alone, lost its mother; he was feeding it by hand. He had been keeping it in the house for several days. As he stooped over it in the yard, with a vessel of new milk he had obtained, with which to feed it, my master came along, and without the least provocation, began by asking,

Master: "Bazil, have you fed the flock?"

Bazil: "Yes, sir."

Master: "The fact is, I have too many of you; my people are getting to be the most careless, lazy, and worthless in the country."

Bazil: "Master, I am always at my post; Monday morning never finds me off the plantation."

Master: "Hush! I shall have to sell some of you; and then the rest will have enough to do; I have not work enough to keep you all tightly employed; I have too many of you."

Events in the History of James W. C. Pennington: Formerly a Slave *(cont.)*

James: All this was said in an angry, threatening, and exceedingly insulting tone. My father was a high-spirited man, and feeling deeply the insult, replied to the last expression,

Bazil: "If I am one too many, sir, give me a chance to get a purchaser, and I am willing to be sold when it may suit you."

Master: "I told you to hush!"

James: He drew forth the "cowhide" from under his arm and fell upon my father with most savage cruelty, inflicting fifteen or twenty severe stripes, with all his strength, over his shoulders and the small of his back. As he raised himself upon his toes, and gave the last stripe, he said,

Master: "I will make you know that I am master of your tongue as well as of your time!"

James: I was near enough to hear the insolent words that were spoken to my father, and to hear, see, and even count the savage stripes inflicted upon him.

Let me ask any one of Anglo-Saxon blood and spirit, how would you expect a son to feel at such a sight?

Each member of my family felt the deep insult that had been inflicted upon our head; we talked of it in our nightly gatherings, and showed it in our daily melancholy aspect. The oppressor saw this, and with the heartlessness that was in perfect keeping with the first insult, commenced a series of tauntings, threatenings, and insinuations, with a view to crush the spirit of the whole family.

Although it was sometime after this event before I took the decisive step, yet in my mind and spirit, I never was a *slave* after it.

Events in the History of James W. C. Pennington: Formerly a Slave *(cont.)*

James:
(cont.)   Whenever I thought of the great contrast between my father's employment on that memorable Monday morning (feeding the little lamb) and the barbarous conduct of my master, I could not help despising the abuser; and I believe he discovered it. Many incidents occurred to convince me of this, but there is one I will mention, because it will serve to show the state of feeling that existed between us, and how it served to widen the already open breach.

I was one day shoeing a horse in the shop yard. I had been stooping for some time under the weight of the horse. When I put down the horse's foot, and straightened myself up to rest a moment my eye caught the Master who was watching me. This threw him into a panic of rage; he would have it that I was watching him.

Master: "What are you rolling your eyes at me for, you lazy rascal?"

James: He came down upon me with his cane, and laid on over my shoulders, arms, and legs, about a dozen severe blows, so that my limbs and flesh were sore for several weeks; and then after several other offensive words, left me.

I have seen men and women flogged—I have seen the overseers strike a man with a hayfork—men have been maimed by shooting. Some dispute arose one morning between the overseer and one of the farm hands, when the former made at the slave with a hickory club; the slave taking to his heels, started for the woods; as he was crossing the yard, the overseer turned, snatched his gun which was near, and fired at the flying slave, lodging several shots in the calf of one leg.

One day the Master swore at my mother and threatened to flog her. And it was then, without counsel or advice from any one, I determined to fly. I arranged my little bundle of clothing, and had secreted it at some distance from the house. It was a day of heartache to me. But I distinctly remember

Events in the History of James W. C. Pennington: Formerly a Slave *(cont.)*

James:
(cont.)

the two great difficulties that stood in the way of my flight: I had a father and mother whom I dearly loved,—I had also six sisters and four brothers on the plantation. The question was, shall I hide my purpose from them? Moreover, how will my flight affect them when I am gone? Will they not be suspected? Will not the whole family be sold off as a disaffected family, as is generally the case when one of its members flies?

But a still more trying question was, how can I expect to succeed, I have no knowledge of distance or direction. I know that Pennsylvania is a free state, but I know not where its soil begins, or where that of Maryland ends. Indeed, at this time there was no safety in Pennsylvania, New Jersey, or New York, for a fugitive.

As the day had rapidly worn away, one of my perplexing questions was settled—I had resolved to let no one into my secret; but the other difficulty was now to be met.

Hope, fear, dread, terror, love, sorrow, and deep melancholy were mingled in my mind together when shortly after Noon I sallied forth across the barnyard and into thick and heavy woods.

Background Information

More than other slaves, young male slaves attempted to run away from their owners. At the age of 20, James left Maryland and fled to Pennsylvania. While hiding with a Quaker family, he was formally educated. He went on to become a preacher and an abolitionist.

Extension Suggestion

Think about the reasons slaves would have escaped from their owners. Write a poem based on what you think. In a small group, read your poem aloud. Make sure you practice reading it before you get in your small group.

The Underground Railcar

Melody: "Oh Susanna" by George N. Allen, 1854

I'm on my way to Canada a freeman's rights to share.
The cruel wrongs of Slavery I can no longer bear;
My heart is crush'd within me so while I remain a slave,
That I'm resolved to strike the blow for Freedom or the Grave!
    O Great Father! do thou pity me.
    And help me on to Canada where the panting slave is free!

I've served my Master all my days without the least reward,
And now I'm forc'd to flee away to shun the lash abhor'd;
The hounds are baying on my track, my Master's just behind,
Resolv'd that he will bring me back and fast his fetters bind.
    O Great Father! do thou pity me.
    And help me on to Canada where the panting slave is free!

I've heard that Queen Victoria has pledged us all a home
Beyond the reach of Slavery, if we will only come;
So I have fled this weary way, my guide the bright north star,
And now, thank God, I speed today in the Underground Railcar.
    O old Master! why come after me,
    I'm whizzing fast to Canada where the panting slave is free!

I now embark for yonder shore, sweet land of liberty.
The vessel soon will bear me o'er, and I shall then be free;
No more I'll dread the auctioneer, nor fear the Master's frowns,
No more I'll tremble lest I hear the baying of the hounds.
    O old Master, 'tis vain to follow me.
    I'm just in sight of Canada, where the panting slave is free!

The Underground Railcar *(cont.)*

Yes! I am safe in Canada—my soul and body free.
My blood and tears no more shall drench thy soil, O Tennessee!
Yet how can I suppress the tear that's stealing from my eye,
To think my friends and kindred dear as slaves must live and die.
    O dear friends, haste and follow me,
    For I am safe in Canada, where the panting slave is free!

Background Information

The Underground Railroad was a network of both white and black people who tried to help slaves escape from their masters in the slave states. These people worked together to move the slaves through their communities to Canada where a black man could vote and own land.

Company Aytch (H)

By Sam R. Watkins

Reader mine, did you live in that stormy period?

In the year of our Lord eighteen hundred and sixty-one, do you remember those trying times?

Do you recollect in that year, for the first time in your life, of hearing Dixie and the Bonnie Blue Flag?

Fort Sumter was fired upon from Charleston by troops under General Beauregard, and Major Anderson, of the Federal army, surrendered. The die was cast; war was declared. Lincoln called for troops from Tennessee and all the Southern states, but Tennessee, loyal to Southern sister states passed the ordinance of secession, and enlisted under the Stars and Bars. From that day on every person, almost, was eager for war, and we were all afraid it would be over and we not in the fight. Companies were made up, regiments organized; left, left, left, was heard from morning till night. By the right flank, file left march, were familiar sounds. Everywhere could be seen Southern stockades made by the ladies and our sweethearts. And some who afterwards became Union men made the most fiery secession speeches . . . Flags made by the ladies were presented to companies, and to hear the young orators tell of how they would protect that flag, and that they would come back with the flag or come not at all, and if they fell they would fall with their backs to the field and their feet to the foe, would fairly make our hair stand on end with intense patriotism, and we wanted to march right off and whip twenty Yankees. But we soon found out that the glory of war was at home among the ladies and not upon the field of blood and carnage of death, where our comrades were mutilated and torn by shot and shell. And to see the cheek blanch and to hear the fervent prayer, aye, I might say the agony of mind were very different indeed from the patriotic times at home.

Background Information

Sam R. Watkins, from Columbia, Tennessee, joined the First Tennessee Regiment, Company H, to fight for the Confederacy. Of the 120 original recruits in his company, Watkins was one of only seven to survive every one of its battles. Twenty years later, he wrote this remarkable account of the company. The contrast of patriotism before joining the war and the reality of the war itself comes through in this piece.

#50113—Building Fluency through Practice and Performance   © *Shell Education*

Voices from the Civil War

Compiled by Timothy Rasinski

Background Information

This selection of voices from the Civil War shows different viewpoints concerning what led up to the war, the war in action, and the reuniting and healing of the United States. This selection is divided into three segments.

Prelude to War
Secession, Rebellion, War
One Nation Again

Directions

This is a reader's theater for a pair of students. One student reads the bold type. Then, the other student reads the quotation. After you finish each of the three segments, think about what was read. How are the voices similar? How are they different?

Part 1—Prelude to War

Virginia Declaration of Rights, June 1776

"That all men are by nature equally free and independent, and have certain inherent rights."

Declaration of Independence, July 1776

"We hold these truths to be self-evident, that all men are created equal, that they are endowed by their Creator with certain unalienable Rights, that among these are Life, Liberty, and the pursuit of Happiness."

Abraham Lincoln, April 1859

"All honor to Jefferson—to the man who, in the concrete pressure of a struggle for national independence, had the coolness, forecast, and capacity to introduce . . . an abstract truth, applicable to all men and all times."

Amendment X, Constitution of the United States, 1791

"The powers not delegated to the United States by the Constitution, nor prohibited by it to the states, are reserved to the states respectively, or to the people."

Voices from the Civil War *(cont.)*

Part 1—Prelude to War *(cont.)*

Frederick Douglass

"In thinking of America, I sometimes find myself admiring her bright blue sky, her grand old woods, her fertile fields, her beautiful rivers, her mighty lakes and star-crowned mountains. But my rapture is soon checked, my joy is soon turned to mourning. When I remember that all is cursed with the infernal spirit of slave-holding and wrong; When I remember that with the waters of her noblest rivers, the tears of my brethren are borne to the ocean, disregarded and forgotten; That her most fertile fields drink daily of the warm blood of my outraged sisters, I am filled with unutterable loathing, and led to reproach myself that anything could fall from my lips in praise of such a land."

Abraham Lincoln, June 1858

"In my opinion, it will not cease, until a crisis shall have been reached and passed. 'A house divided against itself cannot stand.' I believe this government cannot endure permanently half slave and half free. I do not expect the Union to be dissolved—I do not expect the house to fall—but I do expect it will cease to be divided. It will become all one thing or all the other."

"Either the opponents of slavery, will arrest the further spread of it, and place it where the public mind shall rest in the belief that it is in the course of ultimate extinction; or its advocates will push it forward, till it shall become alike lawful in all the States, old as well as new—North as well as South."

Senator Stephen Douglas, First Lincoln-Douglas Debate, August 1858

"I do not question Mr. Lincoln's conscientious belief that the Negro was made his equal and hence is his brother, but for my own part, I do not regard the Negro as my equal, and positively deny that he is my brother or any kin to me whatever."

John Brown, December 1859

"I, John Brown, am now quite certain that the crimes of this guilty land will never be purged away but with blood."

#50113—Building Fluency through Practice and Performance © *Shell Education*

Voices from the Civil War *(cont.)*

Part 1—Prelude to War *(cont.)*

William Lloyd Garrison

"Wherever there is a human being, I see God-given rights inherent in that being, whatever the sex or complexion."

John Brown, 1859

"I pity the poor in bondage that have none to help them; that is why I am here; not to gratify any personal animosity, revenge, or vindictive spirit. It is my sympathy with the oppressed and the wronged, that are as good as you, and as precious in the sight of God."

Abraham Lincoln, February 1860

"Neither let us be slandered from our duty by false accusations against us, nor frightened from it by menaces of destruction to the Government nor of dungeons to ourselves. LET US HAVE FAITH THAT RIGHT MAKES MIGHT, AND IN THAT FAITH, LET US, TO THE END, DARE TO DO OUR DUTY AS WE UNDERSTAND IT."

William Lloyd Garrison

"The success of any great moral enterprise does not depend upon numbers."

Henry David Thoreau, October 1859

"I hear many condemn these men because they were so few. When were the good and the brave ever in a majority? Would you have had him wait till that time came?—'til you and I came over to him? The very fact that John Brown had no rabble or troop of hirelings about him would alone distinguish him from ordinary heroes. His company was small indeed, because few could be found worthy to pass muster."

John Brown, 1859

"I wish to say, furthermore, that you had better, all you people of the South, prepare yourselves for a settlement of that question, that must come up for settlement sooner than you are prepared for it. The sooner you are prepared the better. You may dispose of me very easily. I am nearly disposed of now; but this question is still to be settled—this Negro question, I mean; the end of that is not yet."

Voices from the Civil War *(cont.)*

Part 1—Prelude to War *(cont.)*

Henry Wadsworth Longfellow, 1859

"This will be a great day in our history; the date of a New Revolution—quite as much needed as the old one. Even now as I write they are leading old John Brown to execution in Virginia for attempting to rescue slaves! This is sowing the wind to reap the whirlwind which will come soon!"

John Brown, Last Public Statement, 1859

"Now if it is deemed necessary that I should forfeit my life for the furtherance of the ends of justice, and mingle my blood with the blood of my children and with the blood of millions in this slave country whose rights are disregarded by wicked, cruel, and unjust enactments—I submit; so let it be done."

Henry David Thoreau, October 1859

"Some eighteen hundred years ago Christ was crucified; this morning, perchance, Captain John Brown was hung. These are the two ends of a chain which is not without its links. He is not Old Brown any longer; he is an angel of light."

Frederick Douglass, 1881

John Brown's "zeal in the cause of freedom was infinitely superior to mine. Mine was as the taper light; his was as the burning sun. I could live for the slave; John Brown could die for him."

Henry David Thoreau, October 1859

"I wish I could say that John Brown was the representative of the North. He was a superior man. He did not value his bodily life in comparison with ideal things. He did not recognize unjust human laws, but resisted them as he was bid. For once we are lifted out of the trivialness and dust of politics into the region of truth and manhood. No man in America has ever stood up so persistently and effectively for the dignity of human nature, knowing himself for a man, and the equal of any and all governments. In that sense he was the most American of us all."

William Lloyd Garrison

"In firing his gun, John Brown has merely told what time of day it is. It is high noon."

#50113—Building Fluency through Practice and Performance © Shell Education

Voices from the Civil War *(cont.)*

Part 2—Secession, Rebellion, War

President Jefferson Davis, Confederate States of America, Inaugural Address, February 1861

"We have entered upon the career of independence, and it must be inflexibly pursued. As a necessity, not a choice, we have resorted to the remedy of separation: and henceforth our energies must be directed to the conduct of our own affairs, and the perpetuity of the Confederacy which we have formed. But, if this be denied to us, and the integrity of our territory and jurisdiction be assailed, it will but remain for us, with firm resolve, to appeal to arms and invoke the blessing of Providence on a just cause."

President Abraham Lincoln, Inaugural Address, March 1861

"We are not enemies, but friends. We must not be enemies. Though passion may have strained, it must not break our bonds of affection. The mystic chords of memory, stretching from every battlefield and patriot grave, to every living heart and hearthstone, all over this broad land, will yet swell the chorus of the Union, when again touched, as surely they will be, by the better angels of our nature."

President Davis, Inaugural Address, February 1861

"The time for compromise has now passed, and the South is determined to maintain her position, and make all who oppose her smell Southern powder and feel Southern steel."

Lieutenant Colonel Robert E. Lee, United States Army

"There is a terrible war coming, and these young men who have never seen war cannot wait for it to happen, but I tell you, I wish that I owned every slave in the South, for I would free them all to avoid this war."

Sam Houston, Governor of Texas, 1861

"Let me tell you what is coming. After the sacrifice of countless millions of treasure and hundreds of thousands of lives you may win Southern independence, but I doubt it. The North is determined to preserve this Union. They are not a fiery, impulsive people as you are, for they live in colder climates. But when they begin to move in a given direction, they move with the steady momentum and perseverance of a mighty avalanche."

Voices from the Civil War *(cont.)*

Part 2—Secession, Rebellion, War *(cont.)*

Salmon P. Chase, Governor of Ohio

"The Constitution, in all its provisions, looks to an indestructible Union composed of indestructible States."

Confederate General John Bell Hood

"We will fight you to the death. Better to die a thousand deaths than to submit and live under you and your Negro allies."

Confederate General Pierre Beauregard to Union Major Robert Anderson, Fort Sumter, April 1861

"Sir: I am ordered to demand the evacuation of Fort Sumter. All proper facilities will be afforded for the removal of your self and command. The flag which you have upheld so long and with much fortitude, under the most trying circumstances may be saluted by you on taking it down."

Union Major Robert Anderson's Reply, April 1861

"Sir: I have the honor to acknowledge the receipt of your communication demanding the evacuation of this Fort, and to say in reply thereto that it is a demand with which I regret that my sense of honor and my obligations to my Government prevent my compliance . . ."

Oliver Wendell Holmes, 1863

"The first gun that spat its iron insult at Fort Sumter smote every loyal American full in the face."

Union President Abraham Lincoln, April 1861

"Whereas the laws of the United States have been for some time past, and now are opposed, and the execution thereof obstructed, in the states of South Carolina, Georgia, Alabama, Florida, Mississippi, Louisiana, and Texas . . . I, Abraham Lincoln, President of the United States, hereby do call forth the militia of the several States of the Union to suppress said combinations of states and to cause the laws to be duly executed."

Voices from the Civil War *(cont.)*

Part 2—Secession, Rebellion, War *(cont.)*

Walt Whitman, 1861

Beat! Beat! Drums! Blow! Bugles! Blow! . . .

Make even the trestles to shake the dead, where they lie awaiting the hearses,

So strong you thump, O terrible drums—so loud you bugles blow.

Colonel Robert E. Lee, United States Army, April 1861

"With all my devotion to the Union and the feeling of loyalty and duty of an American citizen, I have not been able to make up my mind to raise my hand against my relatives, my children, my home. I have therefore resigned my commission in the army, and save in defense of my native state, with the sincere hope that my poor services may never be needed, I hope I may never be called on to draw my sword."

Union Major Sullivan Ballou, To his wife Sarah, July 1861

(Major Ballou was killed days later in the First Battle of Bull Run.)

My Very Dear Sarah,

The indications are very strong that we shall move in a few days—perhaps tomorrow. Lest I should not be able to write you again, I feel impelled to write a few lines that may fall under your eye when I shall be no more . . . If it is necessary that I should fall on the battlefield for my Country, I am ready. I have no misgivings about, or lack of confidence in the cause in which I am engaged, and my courage does not halt or falter. I know how strongly American Civilization now leans upon the triumph of the Government, and how great a debt we owe to those who went before us through the blood and suffering of the Revolution. And I am willing—perfectly willing—to lay down all my joys in this life, to help maintain this Government, and to pay that debt.

But, my dear wife, when I know that with my own joys I lay down nearly all of yours, and replace them in this life with cares and sorrows—when, after having eaten for long years the bitter fruit of orphanage myself, I must offer it as their only sustenance to my dear little children—is it weak or dishonorable, while the banner of my purpose floats calmly and proudly in the breeze, that my unbounded love for you, my darling wife and children, should struggle in fierce, though useless, contest with my love of Country.

Voices from the Civil War *(cont.)*

Part 2—Secession, Rebellion, War *(cont.)*

Union Major Sullivan Ballou *(cont.)*

Sarah my love for you is deathless, it seems to bind me to you with mighty cables that nothing but Omnipotence could break; and yet my love of Country comes over me like a strong wind, and bears me irresistibly on with all these chains, to the battlefield.

The memories of all the blissful moments I have spent with you come creeping over me, and I feel most gratified to God and you that I have enjoyed them so long. And hard it is for me to give them up and burn to ashes the hopes of future years, when God willing, we might still have lived and loved together, and seen our sons grow up to honorable manhood around us. I have, I know, but few and small claims upon Divine Providence, but something whispers to me—perhaps it is the wafted prayer of my little Edgar, that I shall return to my loved ones unharmed. If I do not, my dear Sarah, never forget how much I love you, and when my last breath escapes me on the battlefield, it will whisper your name. . .

But, O Sarah! if the dead can come back to this earth and flit unseen around those they loved, I shall always be near you; in the garish day and in the darkest night—amidst your happiest scenes and gloomiest hours—always, always; and if there be a soft breeze upon your cheek, it shall be my breath: or the cool air cools your throbbing temple, it shall be my spirit passing by.

Sarah, do not mourn me dead; think I am gone and wait for thee, for we shall meet again.

Stephen Vincent Benet about the Union defeat at Bull Run, from *John Brown's Body*, 1928

All night the Union army fled in retreat
Like horses scared by a shadow—a stumbling flood
Of panicky men who had been brave for a while
And might be brave again on another day
But now were merely children chased by the night
       And each man tainting his neighbor with the same
       Blind fear.

Voices from the Civil War *(cont.)*

Part 2—Secession, Rebellion, War *(cont.)*

Union Brigadier General Ulysses S. Grant, February 1862

"Sir: Yours of this date, proposing armistice and appointment of Commissioners to settle terms of capitulation, is just received. No terms except an unconditional and immediate surrender can be accepted. I propose to move immediately upon your works."

John F. Brobst, 25th Wisconsin Regiment, July 1863

"Grant is the only man that can whip the Rebs every time, and he can do it every time that he tries it. We would not give our General Grant for all the generals that are in the Northern army. When his men go in a fight they know he is going to have us whip them."

Union General Grant

"Find out where your enemy is. Get at him as soon as you can. Strike him as hard as you can, and keep moving on!"

Union President Lincoln, Response to a critic urging the dismissal of General Grant after the Battle of Shiloh, 1862

"I can't spare this man: he fights."

Union General Grant, July 1885

"Shiloh was the severest battle fought at the West during the war. . . I saw an open field. . . so covered with dead that it would have been possible to walk across the clearing in any direction, stepping on dead bodies, without a foot touching the ground."

Confederate General George Pickett, Gettysburg, July 1863

"Up men, and to your posts! Don't forget today that you are from Old Virginia."

Confederate Soldier at Gettysburg, July 1863

"We'll fight them, sir, 'til hell freezes over, and then, sir, we will fight them on the ice."

Voices from the Civil War *(cont.)*

Part 2—Secession, Rebellion, War *(cont.)*

Carl Sandburg, American Poet, From *Abraham Lincoln, The War Years*

"Then came cold steel, the bayonet, the clubbed musket. The strongest and last line of the enemy was reached. 'The Confederate battle flag waved over his defenses,' said a Confederate major, 'and the fighting over the wall became hand to hand, but more than half having already fallen, our line was too weak to route the enemy.'"

Massachusetts private at Gettysburg, July 1863

"The hoarse and indistinguishable orders of commanding officers, the screaming and bursting of shells, canister and shrapnel as they tore through the struggling masses of humanity, the death screams of wounded animals, the groans of their human companions, wounded and dying and trampled underfoot by hurrying batteries, rider-less horses and the moving lines of battle—a perfect Hell on earth, never, perhaps to be equaled, certainly not to be surpassed, nor ever to be forgotten in a man's lifetime. It has never been effaced from my memory, day or night, for fifty years."

Union President Lincoln, Gettysburg Address, November 19, 1863

"It is for us, the living, rather, to be dedicated here to the unfinished work which they who fought here have thus far so nobly advanced. It is rather for us to be here dedicated to the great task remaining before us—that from these honored dead we take increased devotion to that cause for which they gave the last full measure of devotion—that we here highly resolve that these dead shall not have died in vain—that this nation, under God, shall have a new birth of freedom and that government of the people, by the people, for the people, shall not perish from the earth."

Carl Sandburg

"His cadences sang the ancient song that where there is freedom men have fought and sacrificed for it, and that freedom is worth men's dying for. For the first time since he became president, Lincoln had on a dramatic occasion declaimed, howsoever it might be read, Jefferson's proposition which had been a slogan of the Revolutionary War—

'All men are created equal'—leaving no other inference than that he regarded the Negro slave as a man."

Voices from the Civil War *(cont.)*

Part 2—Secession, Rebellion, War *(cont.)*

Black Union Soldier, To his former master, a Confederate prisoner

"Hello, Massa; bottom rail on top dis time."

Union General Benjamin F. Butler

"The colored man fills an equal place in the ranks while he lives and an equal grave when he falls."

Frederick Douglass

"The American people and the Government at Washington may refuse to recognize it for a time but the inexorable logic of events will force it upon them in the end; that the war now being waged is a war for and against slavery."

Union Colonel Joshua Lawrence Chamberlain, Fredericksburg, December 1862

"But out of that silence rose . . . new sounds more appalling still . . . a strange ventriloquism, of which you could not locate the source, a smothered moan . . . as if a thousand discords were flowing together into a key-note weird, unearthly, terrible to hear and bear, yet startling with its nearness; the writhing concord broken by cries for help . . . some begging for a drop of water, some calling on God for pity; and some on friendly hands to finish what the enemy had so horribly begun; some with delirious, dreamy voices murmuring loved names, as if the dearest were bending over them; and underneath, all the time, the deep bass note from closed lips too hopeless, or too heroic to articulate their agony . . . It seemed best to bestow myself between two dead men among the many left there by earlier assaults, and to draw another crosswise for a pillow out of the trampled, blood-soaked sod, pulling the flap of his coat over my face to fend off the chilling winds, and still more chilling, the deep, many voiced moan that overspread the field."

Confederate General Lee, December 1862

"It is well that war is so terrible, or else we should grow too fond of it."

Voices from the Civil War *(cont.)*

Part 2—Secession, Rebellion, War *(cont.)*

Louisa May Alcott, Union army nurse, From *Hospital Sketches*, 1863

"The sight of several stretchers, each with its legless, armless, or desperately wounded occupant, entering my ward, admonished me that I was there to work . . . Round the great stove was gathered the dreariest group I ever saw—ragged, gaunt, and pale, mud to the knees, with bloody bandages untouched since put on days before; many bundled up in blankets, coats being lost or useless; and all wearing that disheartened look which proclaimed defeat."

John F. Brobst, July 1863

"The people up north do not know what war is. If they were to come down here once, they would soon find out the horror of war. Wherever the army goes, they leave nothing behind them, take all the horses, all the cattle, hogs, sheep, chickens, corn and in fact, everything, and the longer the rebs hold out the worse it is for them."

John Trowbridge, Author

"A Confederate brigadier general said to me, 'One could track the line of Sherman's march all through Georgia and South Carolina by the fires on the horizon . . . He stripped our people of everything. He deserves to be called the great robber of the nineteenth century.'"

Union General William Tecumseh Sherman, November 1864

"You cannot qualify war in harsher terms than I will. War is cruelty and you cannot refine it. There is no use trying to reform it. The crueler it is, the sooner it will be over."

Union President Lincoln, March 1865

"Fondly do we hope, fervently do we pray, that this mighty scourge of war may speedily pass away. Yet, if God wills that it continue until all the wealth piled up by the bondsman's two-hundred and fifty years of unrequited toil shall be sunk, until every drop of blood drawn with the lash shall be paid by another drawn with the sword, as was said three thousand years ago, so still it must be said, 'The judgments of the Lord are true and righteous altogether.'"

Voices from the Civil War *(cont.)*

Part 2—Secession, Rebellion, War *(cont.)*

Union General Sherman

"I think I understand what military fame is; to be killed on the field of battle and have your name misspelled in the newspapers."

A Union soldier

"General Grant habitually wears an expression as if he had determined to drive his head through a brick wall and was about to do it."

Confederate General Thomas "Stonewall" Jackson, His dying words, May 10, 1863

"Let us pass over the river and rest under the shade of the trees."

Union General Grant, March 1865

"We are now having fine weather and I think will be able to wind up matters about Richmond soon . . . The rebellion has lost its vitality and if I am not much mistaken there will be no rebel army of any great dimensions in a few weeks hence."

Union President Lincoln, March 1865

"With malice toward none; with charity for all; with firmness in the right, as God gives us to see the right, let us strive on to finish the work we are in; to bind up the nation's wounds; to care for him who shall have borne the battle and for his widow, and his orphan—to do all which may achieve and cherish a just and lasting peace among ourselves, and with all nations."

Union General Grant, April 1865

"When news of the surrender first reached our lines our men commenced firing a salute of a hundred guns in honor of victory. I at once sent word, however, to have it stopped. The Confederates were now our prisoners, and we did not want to exult over their downfall."

Confederate General Lee, April 1865

"After four years of arduous service, marked by unsurpassed courage and fortitude, the Army of Northern Virginia has been compelled to yield to overwhelming numbers and resources."

Voices from the Civil War *(cont.)*

Part 3—One Nation Again

Union General Grant, April 1865

"The war is over. The rebels are our countrymen again."

Union General Chamberlain, On the Confederate surrender at Appomattox Court House, April 1865

". . . On they come, with the old swinging route step and swaying battle flags. In the van, the proud Confederate ensign. Before us in proud humiliation stood the embodiment of manhood; men whom neither toils and sufferings, nor the fact of death could bend from their resolve; standing before us now, thin, worn, and famished, but erect, and with eyes looking level into ours, waking memories that bound us together as no other bond; was not such manhood to be welcomed back into a Union so tested and assured? On our part not a sound of trumpet more, nor roll of drum; not a cheer, nor word, nor whisper or vain-glorying, nor motion of man, but an awed stillness rather, and breath-holding, as if it were the passing of the dead!"

Confederate General Lee

"I have fought against the people of the North because I believe they were seeking to wrest from the South its dearest rights. But I have never cherished toward them bitter or vindictive feelings, and have never seen the day when I did not pray for them."

Union President Lincoln, 1865

"With malice toward none; with charity for all; with firmness in the right, as God gives us to see the right, let us strive on to finish the work we are in; to bind up the nation's wounds; to care for him who shall have borne the battle and for his widow, and his orphan—to do all which may achieve and cherish a just and lasting peace among ourselves, and with all nations."

Union General Grant, April 1865

"Let them hope for perpetual peace and harmony with that enemy, whose manhood, however mistaken the cause, drew forth such Herculean deeds of valor."

#50113—Building Fluency through Practice and Performance © *Shell Education*

Voices from the Civil War *(cont.)*

Part 3—One Nation Again *(cont.)*

Confederate soldier

"We talked the matter over and could have settled the war in thirty minutes had it been left to us."

Confederate General Lee, 1865

"I believe it to be the duty of everyone to unite in the restoration of the country and the reestablishment of peace and harmony."

Sam Watkins, 1st Tennessee, Confederate Army

"America has no north, no south, no east, no west. The sun rises over the hills and sets over the mountains, the compass just points up and down, and we can laugh now at the absurd notion of there being a north and a south. We are one and undivided."

Union President Lincoln, December 1862

"In giving freedom to the slave, we assure freedom to the free—honorable alike in what we give, and what we preserve. We shall nobly save, or meanly lose, the last best hope of earth."

Confederate President Davis, April 1882

"Our cause was so just, so sacred, that had I known all that has come to pass, had I known what was to be inflicted upon me, all that my country was to suffer, all that our posterity was to endure, I would do it all over again."

Union President Lincoln, April 1859

"Those who deny freedom to others deserve it not for themselves; and, under a just God, cannot long retain it."

Union President Lincoln, Gettysburg Address, November 19, 1863

". . . that this nation, under God, shall have a new birth of freedom, and that government of the people, by the people, for the people, shall not perish from the earth."

Voices from the Civil War *(cont.)*

Part 3—One Nation Again *(cont.)*

Frederick Douglass

"Viewing the man from the genuine abolitionist ground, Mr. Lincoln seemed cold, tardy, weak and unequal to the task. But, viewing him from the sentiments of his people, which as a statesman he was bound to respect, then his actions were swift, bold, radical, and decisive. Taking the man in the whole, balancing the tremendous magnitude of the situation, and the necessary means to ends, Infinite Wisdom has rarely sent a man into the world more perfectly suited to his mission than Abraham Lincoln."

Walt Whitman, American Poet, 1865

O Captain, my Captain! our fearful trip is done,
The ship has weather'd every rack, the prize we sought is won.
The port is near, the bells I hear, the people all exulting,
While follow eyes the steady keel, the vessel grim and daring;
But O heart! heart! heart!
O the bleeding drops of red!
Where on the deck my captain lies,
Fallen cold and dead.

John Greenleaf Whittier, American Writer, 1867

It is done!
Clang of bell and roar of gun
Send tidings up and down.
How the belfries rock and reel!
How the great guns, peal on peal,
Fling the joy from town to town!

William Faulkner, American Writer, 1951

"The past is never dead. It's not even past."

#50113—Building Fluency through Practice and Performance © Shell Education

Gettysburg and Mr. Lincoln's Speech

By Timothy Rasinski

A reader's theater for five voices

Narrator 1: The Civil War was a tragic time in America. It pitted the Southern states against the Northern states.

Narrator 2: It also pitted brother against brother and friend against friend.

Northern Soldier: I fight to end slavery and to make our country whole again— although we may come from many states, we are one nation and always will be one nation.

Southern Soldier: I fight against the Northerners who try to impose their will on the South, telling us that we have to put an end to slavery, telling us that we cannot live our lives the way that we wish.

Narrator 1: The war was a bloody one. More American soldiers died in the Civil War than in any other war involving the United States.

Narrator 2: Through the first few years of the Civil War, the Southern, or Confederate, army, under General Robert E. Lee, won battle after battle against the North.

Southern Soldier: One of us Rebels can whip the tar out of ten Yankees!

Northern Soldier: We are good soldiers and we're ready to fight. Our generals, however, are no match for the Confederate generals—Robert E. Lee and Stonewall Jackson.

Narrator 1: In 1863, General Lee felt strong enough to invade Pennsylvania, an important Northern state. By taking the war to the North, Lee thought that he could convince the North to give up its attempt to reunite the states and end slavery.

Narrator 2: At this time, the Union army was under the command of General George Meade. He knew that the army had to stop the Confederates. The armies met during the first three days of July 1863 in a small Pennsylvania town called . . .

All: GETTYSBURG!

Gettysburg and Mr. Lincoln's Speech *(cont.)*

Narrator 1: For three days, under the hot summer sun the two huge armies struggled.

Southern Soldier: Long live the Confederacy!

Northern Soldier: Union forever! Rally 'round the flag, boys!

Narrator 2: The battle swung back and forth over those blistering hot days. It finally ended in a failed attempt by the Confederates to break through the line of Union soldiers.

Southern Soldier: We called it Pickett's Charge. It was a disaster. Thousands of gray-clad soldiers were cut down in the murderous fire coming from the Yankee lines.

Narrator 1: Pickett's Charge failed, and Lee knew he had lost the battle. He knew he had to withdraw his army to Virginia—his home state and friendlier territory.

Narrator 2: And so Lee moved his battered and defeated army from Pennsylvania on July fourth. He had to leave so quickly that many of the dead and wounded Southern soldiers were left lying on the battlefield.

Southern Soldier: We didn't want to leave our fallen brothers lying on Northern soil. But we had to retreat south or risk being annihilated by the victorious Yankees.

Narrator 1: The next day, Meade's army followed Lee out of Pennsylvania, hoping to catch up with him and complete the destruction of the Southern army. He also left many of his dead lying on the battlefield. All told, nearly 50,000 soldiers, Northern and Southern were killed, wounded, or missing at Gettysburg.

Northern Soldier: We tasted sweet victory at last. Now, we wanted to finally put an end to this bloody war. We had to chase the enemy wherever he went.

Narrator 2: But for the people living in Gettysburg, the battle was far from over. When the few thousand residents of Gettysburg returned to their homes, they were greeted by the sight and stench of death.

#50113—Building Fluency through Practice and Performance   *© Shell Education*

Gettysburg and Mr. Lincoln's Speech *(cont.)*

Narrator 1: Imagine the scene—thousands of dead soldiers and animals lying out in the middle of the battlefield and in shallow graves under the broiling July sun. Something had to be done quickly to prevent the spread of disease from all the dead and decaying bodies.

Narrator 2: In previous battles, bodies of dead soldiers were sent to their hometowns for burial.

Narrator 1: But this was not possible at Gettysburg. There were simply too many dead and not enough workers to prepare the bodies for transport home. It would take too long.

Narrator 2: The governor of Pennsylvania then made an important decision: the dead soldiers would be buried in a new cemetery in Gettysburg. Burying the bodies in Gettysburg could be accomplished quickly. The threat from the spread of disease would be averted. All the Northern states were asked to contribute money for the cemetery for the Gettysburg dead.

Northern Soldier: And so, from July to November, in the year 1863, workers gathered the bodies of our fallen comrades and buried them in the new cemetery.

Southern Soldier: Even some of our Southern martyrs were buried at Gettysburg.

Narrator 1: By November, the cemetery was finished. By November, the country understood just how important the Battle of Gettysburg was. No more would the Confederate army threaten the Northern states. The Confederacy had reached its high mark and was now in decline.

Narrator 2: Thus, it was decided that a dedication for the cemetery should take place to honor those Northern soldiers who made the ultimate sacrifice at Gettysburg.

Narrator 1: Dignitaries from around the country were invited. President Lincoln came. The greatest orator, or speechmaker, of the day, Edward Everett, was also asked to give a grand speech. He spoke for over two hours.

Gettysburg and Mr. Lincoln's Speech *(cont.)*

Narrator 2: Those who came to the dedication were tired and wanted to go home by the time Everett had finished his long speech.

Narrator 1: But then, it was President Lincoln's turn to make a few brief remarks.

Narrator 2: Slowly, and so very deliberately, President Lincoln stood up and made his way to the podium. Quietly, he faced the crowd of public dignitaries and ordinary citizens standing in front of him. Somberly, he looked over the countless rows of dead soldiers behind him. And, in just 272 words, Mr. Lincoln helped all of us, those living in 1863 and those of us alive today, understand what is special about our country and why it could not be broken up into free and slave, Union and Confederate, North and South.

(Pause for effect.)

Lincoln: *Four score and seven years ago, our fathers brought forth on this continent, a new nation, conceived in liberty, and dedicated to the proposition that all men are created equal.*

Narrator 1: Lincoln uses words from the Declaration of Independence to remind us why the United States was founded in the first place.

Lincoln: *Now we are engaged in a great civil war, testing whether that nation, or any nation so conceived and so dedicated, can long endure. We are met on a great battlefield of that war. We have come to dedicate a portion of that field, as a final resting place for those who here gave their lives that the nation might live. It is altogether fitting and proper that we should do this.*

But in a larger sense, we cannot dedicate, we cannot consecrate, we cannot hallow this ground. The brave men, living and dead, who struggled here, have consecrated it, far beyond our poor power to add or detract.

Narrator 2: Although the dedication at which Lincoln was speaking was meant to make this land special, Lincoln knew, and he told the audience, that the brave soldiers who fought here that summer had made it much more special through their actions than by anything Lincoln could say or do.

Gettysburg and Mr. Lincoln's Speech (cont.)

Lincoln: *The world will little note nor long remember what we say here. But it can never forget what they did here.It is for us the living, rather, to be dedicated here to the unfinished work which they who fought here have thus far so nobly advanced. It is rather for us to be here dedicated to the great task remaining before us. That from these honored dead we take increased devotion to that cause for which they gave the last full measure of devotion.*

Narrator 1: Although the soldiers who died here saved the Union, much fighting and hard work still need to be done before the nation can be whole again.

Narrator 2: Lincoln realized that the United States was a grand and never-before-tried experiment for all the world to see—Can a government created by its citizens and run by its citizens truly work? The world was watching and waiting to find out.

Lincoln: *That we here highly resolve that these dead shall not have died in vain. That this nation, under God, shall have a new birth of freedom. And that . . .*

All: **Government of the people, by the people, for the people, shall not perish from the earth.**

Background Information

President Lincoln delivered the Gettysburg Address on November 19, 1863. The battlefield was to become a national cemetery. This was its dedication ceremony.

The Early Twentieth Century

#50113—Building Fluency through Practice and Performance

Carl Sandburg on World War I

By Lorraine Griffith

A reader's theater for four voices: three readers (R) and Carl Sandburg (CS)

R1: Carl Sandburg was a famous American poet who was inspired by the history of America.

R2: Like people today, he had mixed feelings about war and patriotism.

R3: He honored those who gave their lives for freedom during World War I,

R1: but yet struggled with how easily people seemed to accept the loss of life.

R1: In this poem by Sandburg, written in 1914, he describes a boy in a newspaper office moving buttons. These buttons represented the fronts of the war moving across Europe.

R2: He contrasts the easy movement of various colored buttons with the thousands of dead bodies left in the aftermath of battle.

R3: Listen now as Carl Sandburg reads his poem, "Buttons."

CS: *I have been watching the war map slammed up for*
advertising in front of the newspaper office.
Buttons—red and yellow buttons—blue and black buttons—
are shoved back and forth across the map.

A laughing young man, sunny with freckles,
Climbs a ladder, yells a joke to somebody in the crowd,
And then fixes a yellow button one inch west
And follows the yellow button with a black button one inch west.

R1–R3: *(Ten thousand men and boys twist their bodies in a red soak*
along a river edge,

Carl Sandburg on World War I *(cont.)*

R1:   *Gasping of wounds,*

R2:   *calling for water,*

R3:   *some rattling death in their throats.)*

CS: *Who would guess what it cost to move two buttons one inch on the war map here in front of the newspaper office where the freckle-faced young man is laughing to us?*

R1:   Two buttons

R2:   One inch

R3:   Who would guess

All: **What it cost?**

Background Information

World War I was called many names: the First World War, the War to End All Wars, and The Great War. This world war was fought in Europe between 1914 and 1918. The United States entered the war in 1917.

Voices from the Great Depression

Compiled by Wendy Conklin

Stock Exchange Guard, October 29, 1929

"They roared like a lot of lions and tigers. They hollered and screamed, they clawed at one another's collars. It was like a bunch of crazy men. Every once in a while, when Radio or Steel or Auburn would take another tumble, you'd see some poor devil collapse and fall to the floor."

President Herbert Hoover, Speaks on unemployment

"Many people have left their jobs for the more profitable one of selling apples."

Unemployed Coal Miner in Kentucky

"We have been eating such weeds as cows eat."

A Pennsylvania Man

"This is the first time in my life that I have asked for help, but the way things are now I must. I have been out of work for a long time and my wife is sick in bed and needs medicine, and no money to buy nothing to eat and what is a fellow going to do. I don't want to steal but I won't let my wife and boy cry for something to eat."

A Philadelphia Storekeeper

"Eleven children in that house. They've got no shoes, no pants. In the house, no chairs. My God, you go in there, you cry, that's all."

President Hoover on Poverty

"We have not yet reached the goal but . . . we shall soon, with the help of God, be in sight of the day when poverty shall be banished from this nation."

President Hoover on the Election, 1932

"This campaign is more than a contest between two men. It is more than a contest between two parties. It is a contest between two philosophies of government."

Voices from the Great Depression *(cont.)*

Evalyn Walsh McLean, Wife of the owner of *The Washington Post*, June 1932

"I saw a dusty automobile truck roll slowly past my house. I saw the unshaven, tired faces of the men who were riding in it standing up. A few were seated at the rear with their legs dangling over the lowered tailboard. On the side of the truck was an expanse of white cloth on which, crudely lettered in black, was a legend, BONUS ARMY.

"Other trucks followed in a straggling succession, and on the sidewalks of Massachusetts Avenue where stroll most of the diplomats and the other fashionables of Washington were some ragged hikers, wearing scraps of old uniforms. The sticks with which they strode along seemed less canes than cudgels. They were not a friendly-looking lot, and I learned they were hiking and riding into the capital along each of its radial avenues; that they had come from every part of the continent."

Franklin Delano Roosevelt, On the day he was elected president

"I'm just afraid that I may not have the strength to do this job."

President Roosevelt, March 4, 1933

"So, first of all, let me assert my firm belief that the only thing we have to fear is fear itself—nameless, unreasoning, unjustified terror which paralyzes needed efforts to convert retreat into advance."

President Franklin Delano Roosevelt

"Do something. And when you have done that something, if it works, do it some more. And if it does not work, then do something else."

John Simpson, President of the National Farmer's Union

"For a farmer to buy a toothbrush, he would have to sell eight dozen eggs and he then would owe two cents. A farmer must sell forty pounds of cotton to buy a good shirt."

Voices from the Great Depression *(cont.)*

Langston Hughes, Poet during the Great Depression

"The Depression brought everybody down a peg or two. And the Negro had but few pegs to fall."

Oklahoma Migrant Worker

"Dust storms and crop failure and such times were rough but word had gotten around there was plenty of work in California, where the money grew on trees."

Dorothea Lange, Photographer, March 1936

"I saw and approached the hungry and desperate mother, as if drawn by a magnet. I do not remember how I explained my presence or my camera to her, but I do remember she asked me no questions. I made five exposures, working closer and closer from the same direction. I did not ask her name or her history. She told me her age, that she was 32. She said that they had been living on frozen vegetables from the surrounding fields, and birds that the children killed. She had just sold the tires from her car to buy food. There she sat in that lean-to tent with her children huddled around her, and seemed to know that my pictures might help her, and so she helped me. There was a sort of equality about it."

First Lady Eleanor Roosevelt, February 7, 1933

"Letters, and letters and letters! Wire baskets on my desk, suitcases of mail going home even on Sundays with my secretary, Mrs. Scheider. A sense of being snowed under by mail. This is a picture of our first few weeks in Washington."

A 9-year-old Pennsylvania Girl

"There are nine of us in the family. My father is out of work for a couple of months and we haven't got a thing to eat in the house . . . I go to school each day. My other sister hain't got any shoes or clothes to wear to go to school. My mother goes in her bare feet and she cries every night that we don't have the help."

Voices from the Great Depression *(cont.)*

A 13-year-old Arkansas Girl, November 6, 1936

"Dear Mrs. Roosevelt, I am writing to you for some of your old soiled dresses if you have any. I am in the seventh grade but I have to stay out of school because I have no books or clothes to ware. I am in need of dresses & slips and a coat very bad. If you have any soiled clothes that you don't want to ware I would be very glad to get them. But please do not let the news paper reporters get hold of this in any way and I will keep it from getting out here so there will be no one else to get hold of it. But do not let my name get out in the paper. I am thirteen years old."

A 15-year-old Girl

"Mrs. Roosevelt, don't think I am just begging, but that is all you can call it I guess. There is no harm in asking I guess either. Do you have any old clothes you have throwed back. You don't realize how honored I would feel to be wearing your clothes. I don't have a coat at all to wear. The clothes may be too large but I can cut them down so I can wear them. Not only clothes but old shoes, hats, hose, and under wear would be appreciated so much. I have three brothers that would appreciate any old clothes of your boys or husband. I wish you could see the part of North Alabama now. The trees, groves, and every thing is covered with ice and snow. It is a very pretty scene. But Oh, how cold it is here. People can hardly stay comfortable."

A 10-year-old Wisconsin Girl, January 9, 1934

"Dear Mrs. F. Roosevelt, I suppose you'll be kind of surprised to hear from a poor little girl. I am ten years old. On Christmas Eve I had wished for Santa Clause to come but my mama said the chimney was blocked & he couldn't come, so I had a poor Christmas. I was expecting Santa to bring me some things. I lost my daddy when I was two years old. I have read in the papers how good you are to the poor and thought maybe you can help me some. I will appreciate it all my life. To-day we have started school from our Christmas vacation & all the children talk about how many presents Santa has brought them & I felt so bad cause I had nothing to say. I guess that is all."

Voices from the Great Depression *(cont.)*

First Lady Eleanor Roosevelt, February 7, 1933

"To give you some idea of the type of thing which comes to my desk and how it is handled, let me tell you a story of a letter written on six sheets of cheap pad paper. It was a mother's story of her family. She spoke well of her husband but he had been unfortunate. They lived in a poor part of the country; a part-time job which the father held had been lost; the land was poor and produced little; their cow had died, and there were five children to be fed and clothed and then one of them, a little fellow of some five years old, had infantile paralysis. He lived, but one leg was badly crippled. How was he going to meet life? She had heard of Warm Springs, but she could not take the trip and she could not pay for the care. What could she do?

"The letter rang true, but I asked a friend to visit them and find out if circumstances were as she described them. They were, and then with the aid of some friends, a fund was raised which paid for the small boy for the long months that he had to stay in Warm Springs; for his trip and for one older person to make the trip with him and settle him there. He stayed until the doctors felt that they could do nothing more for him. When he went home he was sufficiently improved to go to school with the others. He learned to get about on crutches even to walk on them the half mile to and from school every day.

"The years that followed were a gallant fight on the boy's part and on the part of the parents. Finally they had an opportunity to move to a government homestead where the land promised a better living. They were pioneering again in much the same way that their ancestors had done and things looked brighter. At Christmas time last year, the mother wrote me, not a letter of appeal, but the story of a modern pioneering family!"

Background Information

What is known as the Great Depression began with the Stock Market Crash in the United States on October 29, 1929. This day is also called Black Tuesday. The economic downturn of the Great Depression also affected other countries in the world. The depression lasted until the United States entered World War II in 1941.

Duty, Honor, Country: Excerpts from Douglas MacArthur's Farewell to West Point, May 1962

Yours is the profession of arms, the will to win, the sure knowledge that in war there is no substitute for victory, that if you lose, the Nation will be destroyed, that the very obsession of your public service must be duty, honor, country.

These great national problems are not for your professional participation or military solution.

The long, gray line has never failed us. Were you to do so, a million ghosts in olive drab, in brown khaki, in blue and gray, would rise from their white crosses, thundering those magic words: duty, honor, country.

This does not mean that you are warmongers. On the contrary, the soldier, above all other people, prays for peace, for he must suffer and bear the deepest wounds and scars of war. But always in our ears ring the ominous words of Plato, that wisest of all philosophers: "Only the dead have seen the end of war."

The shadows are lengthening for me. The twilight is here. My days of old have vanished—tone and tints. They have gone glimmering through the dreams of things that were. Their memory is one of wondrous beauty, watered by tears and coaxed and caressed by the smiles of yesterday. I listen then, but with thirsty ear, for the witching melody of faint bugles blowing reveille, of far drums beating the long roll.

In my dreams I hear again the crash of guns, the rattle of musketry, the strange, mournful mutter of the battlefield. But in the evening of my memory I come back to West Point. Always there echoes and re-echoes: duty, honor, country.

Today marks my final roll call with you. But I want you to know that when I cross the river, my last conscious thoughts will be of the corps, and the corps, and the corps.

I bid you farewell.

#50113—Building Fluency through Practice and Performance © Shell Education

Duty, Honor, Country: Excerpts from Douglas MacArthur's Farewell to West Point, May 1962

Background Information

One of the most decorated soldiers in American history was Douglas MacArthur. He fought in World War I, World War II and the Korean War. When his career ended in the 1960s, he made a final trip to West Point, the military college of the United States, where he had begun his career. There he addressed the corps of cadets with this speech on what it means to be an American soldier.

Performance Suggestion

Practice and perform this speech as a monologue. Pause in between sentences and paragraphs for effect. In a small group, discuss what MacArthur meant by his repeated phrase, "Duty, Honor, Country." By discussing this phrase, you may be able to say that line with more expression.

America's Voices for Equality

Remember the Ladies

*A reader's theater for six voices: one narrator (N),
three females (F), and two males (M)*

N: This is an exchange of letters between Abigail Adams and her husband, John Adams. John was working with Benjamin Franklin and Thomas Jefferson on a draft of the Declaration of Independence in the spring of 1776. Abigail was very concerned that the new laws would not do anything to increase the freedoms of the ladies in society. ABIGAIL ADAMS TO JOHN ADAMS, MARCH 31, 1776

F1: I long to hear that you have declared an independency. And, by the way, in the new code of laws which I suppose it will be necessary for you to make, I desire you would remember the ladies and be more generous and favorable to them than your ancestors.

F2: Do not put such unlimited power into the hands of the husbands.

F3: Remember, all men would be tyrants if they could. If particular care and attention is not paid to the ladies, we are determined to foment a rebellion, and will not hold ourselves bound by any laws in which we have no voice or representation.

F1: That your sex are naturally tyrannical is a truth so thoroughly established as to admit of no dispute; but such of you as wish to be happy willingly give up—the harsh tide of master for the more tender and endearing one of friend.

F2: Why, then, not put it out of the power of the vicious and the lawless to use us with cruelty and indignity with impunity?

F3: Men of sense in all ages abhor those customs which treat us only as the (servants) of your sex; regard us then as being placed by Providence under your protection, and in imitation of the Supreme Being make use of that power only for our happiness.

N: JOHN ADAMS TO ABIGAIL ADAMS, APRIL 14, 1776

M1: As to your extraordinary code of laws, I cannot but laugh.

M2: We have been told that our struggle has loosened the bonds of government everywhere; that children and apprentices were disobedient; that schools and colleges were grown turbulent; that Indians slighted their guardians, and Negroes grew insolent to their masters.

Remember the Ladies *(cont.)*

M1: But your letter was the first intimation that another tribe, more numerous and powerful than all the rest, were grown discontented.

M2: This is rather too coarse a compliment, but you are so saucy, I won't blot it out.

M1: Depend upon it, we know better than to repeal our masculine systems. Although they are in full force, you know they are little more than theory. We dare not exert our power in its full latitude. We are obliged to go fair and softly, and, in practice, you know we are the subjects.

M2: We have only the name of masters, and rather than give up this, which would completely subject us to the despotism of the petticoat, I hope General Washington and all our brave heroes would fight.

N: ABIGAIL ADAMS TO JOHN ADAMS, MAY 7, 1776

F1: I cannot say that I think you are very generous to the ladies; for, whilst you are proclaiming peace and good-will to men, emancipating all nations, you insist upon retaining an absolute power over wives.

F2: But you must remember that arbitrary power is like most other things which are very hard, very liable to be broken; and, notwithstanding all your wise laws and maxims, we have it in our power, not only to free ourselves,

F3: but to subdue our masters, and without violence, throw both your natural and legal authority at our feet.

Background Information

At the time that Abigail Adams wrote to her husband, women and men were not treated equally by law. Abigail believed women should be educated and should be allowed to vote. She used bold language to express her views, which were beyond her time.

A Declaration of Sentiments

Seneca Falls Conference, New York, 1848

When, in the course of human events, it becomes necessary for one portion of the family of man to assume among the people of the earth a position different from that which they have hitherto occupied, but one to which the laws of nature and of nature's God entitle them, a decent respect to the opinions of mankind requires that they should declare the causes that impel them to such a course.

We hold these truths to be self-evident: that all men and women are created equal; that they are endowed by their Creator with certain inalienable rights, that among these are life, liberty, and the pursuit of happiness; that to secure these rights governments are instituted, deriving their just powers from the consent of the governed. Whenever any form of government becomes destructive of these ends, it is the right of those who suffer from it to refuse allegiance to it, and to insist upon the institution of a new government, laying its foundation on such principles, and organizing its powers in such form as to them shall seem most likely to effect their safety and happiness. Prudence, indeed, will dictate that governments long established should not be changed for light and transient causes; and accordingly, all experience hath shown that mankind are more disposed to suffer, while evils are sufferable, than to right themselves by abolishing the forms to which they are accustomed. But when a long train of abuses and usurpations, pursuing invariably the same object, evinces a design to reduce them under absolute despotism, it is their duty to throw off such government and to provide new guards for their future security. Such has been the patient sufferance of the women under this government, and such is now the necessity which constrains them to demand the equal station to which they are entitled.

The history of mankind is a history of repeated injuries and usurpations on the part of man toward woman, having in direct object the establishment of an absolute tyranny over her. To prove this, let facts be submitted to a candid world.

He has never permitted her to exercise her inalienable right to the elective franchise.

He has compelled her to submit to laws, in the formation of which she had no voice.

He has withheld from her rights which are given to the most ignorant and degraded men—both natives and foreigners.

A Declaration of Sentiments *(cont.)*

Having deprived her of this first right of a citizen, the elective franchise, thereby leaving her without representation in the halls of legislation, he has oppressed her on all sides.

He has made her, if married, in the eye of the law, civilly dead.

He has taken from her all right in property, even to the wages she earns.

He has made her, morally, an irresponsible being, as she can commit many crimes with impunity, provided they be done in the presence of her husband. In the covenant of marriage, she is compelled to promise obedience to her husband, he becoming, to all intents and purposes, her master—the law giving him power to deprive her of her liberty, and to administer chastisement.

He has so framed the laws of divorce, as to what shall be the proper causes of divorce; in case of separation, to whom the guardianship of the children shall be given; as to be wholly regardless of the happiness of women—the law, in all cases, going upon the false supposition of the supremacy of man, and giving all power into his hands.

After depriving her of all rights as a married woman, if single and the owner of property, he has taxed her to support a government which recognizes her only when her property can be made profitable to it.

He has monopolized nearly all the profitable employments, and from those she is permitted to follow, she receives but a scanty remuneration.

He closes against her all the avenues to wealth and distinction, which he considers most honorable to himself. As a teacher of theology, medicine, or law, she is not known.

He has denied her the facilities for obtaining a thorough education—all colleges being closed against her.

He allows her in Church as well as State, but a subordinate position, claiming Apostolic authority for her exclusion from the ministry, and, with some exceptions, from any public participation in the affairs of the Church.

A Declaration of Sentiments *(cont.)*

He has created a false public sentiment, by giving to the world a different code of morals for men and women, by which moral delinquencies which exclude women from society, are not only tolerated but deemed of little account in man.

He has usurped the prerogative of Jehovah himself, claiming it as his right to assign for her a sphere of action, when that belongs to her conscience and to her God.

He has endeavored, in every way that he could, to destroy her confidence in her own powers, to lessen her self-respect, and to make her willing to lead a dependent and abject life.

Now, in view of this entire disfranchisement of one-half the people of this country, their social and religious degradation—in view of the unjust laws above mentioned, and because women do feel themselves aggrieved, oppressed, and fraudulently deprived of their most sacred rights, we insist that they have immediate admission to all the rights and privileges which belong to them as citizens of these United States.

Background Information

This declaration was adopted at a women's rights convention held in Seneca Falls, New York, in July 1848. It is one of the first official declarations of the rights of women in America.

Excerpts from the Emancipation Proclamation

By Abraham Lincoln, President of the United States

A Proclamation.

Whereas, on the twenty-second day of September, in the year of our Lord one thousand eight hundred and sixty-two a proclamation was issued by the President of the United States, containing, among other things, the following, to wit:

That on the first day of January, in the year of our Lord one thousand eight hundred and sixty-three, all persons held as slaves within any state or designated part of a state, the people whereof shall then be in rebellion against the United States, shall be then, thenceforward, and forever free; and the Executive Government of the United States, including the military and naval authority thereof, will recognize and maintain the freedom of such persons, and will do no act or acts to repress such persons, or any of them, in any efforts they may make for their actual freedom.

. . . And by virtue of the power and for the purpose aforesaid, I do order and declare that all persons held as slaves within said designated States, and parts of States are and henceforward shall be free; and that the Executive government of the United States, including the military and naval authorities thereof, will recognize and maintain the freedom of said persons.

And I hereby enjoin upon the people so declared to be free to abstain from all violence, unless in necessary self-defense; and I recommend to them that in all cases when allowed, they labor faithfully for reasonable wages.

And I further declare and make known, that such persons of suitable condition, will be received into the armed services of the United States to garrison forts, positions, stations, and other places, and to man vessels of all sorts in said service.

Excerpts from the Emancipation Proclamation *(cont.)*

And upon this act sincerely believed to be an act of justice, warranted by the Constitution, upon military necessity, I invoke the considerate judgment of mankind, and the gracious favor of Almighty God.

In witness whereof, I have hereunto set my hand and caused the seal of the United States to be affixed.

Done at the City of Washington, this first day of January, in the year of our Lord one thousand eight hundred and sixty three, and of the Independence of the United States of America the eighty-seventh.

Background Information

The Emancipation Proclamation freed the slaves in the South. It took effect on January 1, 1863. Beginning that year, many African Americans began fighting for the North.

Performance Suggestion

Practice and perform the Emancipation Proclamation individually or in small groups. Discuss the meaning of the proclamation and the effect it had on Americans in 1863.

Emancipation

By Paul Laurence Dunbar

Fling out your banners, your honors be bringing,
Raise to the ether your paeans of praise.
Strike every chord and let music be ringing!
Celebrate freely this day of all days.

Few are the years since that notable blessing,
Raised you from slaves to the powers of men.
Each year has seen you my brothers progressing,
Never to sink to that level again.

Perched on your shoulders sits Liberty smiling,
Perched where the eyes of the nations can see.
Keep from her pinions all contact defiling;
Show by your deeds what you're destined to be.

Press boldly forward nor waver, nor falter.
Blood has been freely poured out in your cause,
Lives sacrificed upon Liberty's alter.
Press to the front, it were craven to pause.

Look to the heights that are worth your attaining
Keep your feet firm in the path to the goal.
Toward noble deeds every effort be straining.
Worthy ambition is food for the soul!

#50113—Building Fluency through Practice and Performance　　　© *Shell Education*

Emancipation *(cont.)*

Up! Men and brothers, be noble, be earnest!
Ripe is the time and success is assured;
Know that your fate was the hardest and sternest
When through those lash-ringing days you endured.

Never again shall the manacles gall you
Never again shall the whip stroke defame!
Nobles and Freemen, your destinies call you
Onward to honor, to glory and fame.

Background Information

Paul Laurence Dunbar was one of the first well-known African American poets. The son of former slaves, Dunbar wrote of the African American experience after the Civil War.

Extension Suggestion

Begin by highlighting words in this poem that you do not understand. Work with partners to find the meanings to these words and talk about them. Discuss the feelings Dunbar tried to portray through his words. Has America lived up to the promise suggested by Dunbar in his poem?

It Makes My Heart Sick: Chief Joseph Speaks

Edited by Stephen Griffith;
Arranged by Stephen and Lorraine Griffith

Part 1: A Promise We've Never Broken

A reader's theater for three voices

Narrator: In the 1800s, the Nez Percé was a peaceful nation that spread from Idaho to Northern Washington. Chief Joseph, known by his people as Hin-mah-too-yah-lat-kekt (Thunder coming up over the land from the water), was a well-respected leader of the tribe and had this to say about the tribe's early history:

Reader 1: The first white men of your people who came to our country were named Lewis and Clark. They brought many things which our people had never seen. They talked straight and our people gave them a great feast as proof that our hearts were friendly. They made presents to our chiefs and our people made presents to them . . . .

Reader 2: All [of our tribe], the Nez Percé, made friends with Lewis and Clark and agreed to let them pass through our country and never to make war on white men. This promise the Nez Percé has never broken.

Reader 1: For a short time, we lived quietly. But this could not last. White men had found gold in the mountains around the land of the Winding Water. They stole a great many horses from us . . . and the white men told lies for each other. They drove off a great many of our cattle.

Reader 2: Some white men branded our young cattle so they could claim them. We had no friends who would plead our cause before the law councils. It seemed some of the white men in Wallowa were doing these things on purpose to get up a war. They knew we were not strong enough to fight them.

It Makes My Heart Sick:
Chief Joseph Speaks *(cont.)*

Part 1: A Promise We've Never Broken *(cont.)*

Reader 1: I labored hard to avoid trouble and bloodshed. We gave up some of our country to the white men, thinking that then we could have peace. We were mistaken. The white men would not let us alone. We could have avenged our wrongs many times, but we did not. When the white men were few and we were strong, we could have killed them off, but the Nez Percé wishes to live at peace.

Reader 2: Some of the white men were good, and we lived on peaceful terms with them, but they were not all good. White men claimed my lands and we were ordered to the reservation, but we always replied that we were satisfied to be living on our land. We were careful to refuse the presents and money offered.

Reader 1: Through all the years since the white man came . . . we have been threatened and taunted by them. They have given us no rest. We have had a few good friends among the white men, and they have always advised my people to bear these taunts without fighting. Our young men are quick tempered, and I have had great trouble in keeping them from doing rash things. I have carried a heavy load on my back ever since I was a boy.

Reader 2: We were like deer.

Reader 1: The white men were like grizzly bears.

Reader 2: We had a small country.

Reader 1: Their country was large.

Reader 2: We were contented to let things remain as the Great Spirit Chief made them.

Reader 1: They were not; and would change the mountains and rivers if they did not suit them.

It Makes My Heart Sick:
Chief Joseph Speaks *(cont.)*

Part 2: I Will Fight No More Forever
A reader's theater for two voices

Narrator: Protesting the fraudulent sale of their land, Chief Joseph and his Nez Percé tribe refused to give up their territory in Oregon after the American Civil War. Threatened with forcible removal, they tried to escape to Canada while desperately fighting off the U.S. Army in a war noted for brilliant military maneuvers by the tribe. After traveling more than 1,000 miles over rugged terrain, the outnumbered Nez Percé were captured about thirty miles from Canada. In bitterly cold weather with five inches of snow on the ground, Chief Joseph made this poignant address at his surrender to American forces in the Bear Paw Mountains in 1877.

Chief Joseph: *I am tired of fighting. Our chiefs are killed . . . . The old men are all dead. It is the young men who now say yes or no. He who led the young men is dead. It is cold and we have no blankets. The little children are freezing to death. My people, some of them, have run away to the hills and have no blankets and no food. No one knows where they are— perhaps freezing to death. I want to have time to look for my children and see how many of them I can find. Maybe I shall find them among the dead.*

Hear me, my chiefs. I am tired; my heart is sick and sad. From where the sun now stands I will fight no more forever.

It Makes My Heart Sick:
Chief Joseph Speaks *(cont.)*

Part 3: Good Words and Broken Promises, Washington, D.C., 1879

A reader's theater for one narrator and four readers

Narrator: Chief Joseph was never allowed to return to his Nez Percé homeland even though he was promised he could live in Idaho. He tried every possible appeal to the federal authorities to return the Nez Percé to the land of their ancestors. Making his appeal to leaders in Washington, D.C., he came to the following conclusion:

Reader 1: I have come to Washington, D.C.
There are some things I want to know which no one seems able to explain.

Reader 2: *I cannot understand how the Government sends a man out to fight us and then he breaks his word.*

Reader 3: *Such a government has something wrong about it.*

Reader 4: *I cannot understand why so many* [people] *are allowed to talk so many different ways, and promise so many different things . . . they all say they are my friends, and that I shall have justice, but while all their mouths talk right I do not understand why nothing is done for my people.*

Reader 1: *I have heard talk and talk but nothing is done. Good words do not last long unless they amount to something.*

Reader 2: *Words do not pay for my dead people. They do not pay for my country now overrun by white men. They do not protect my father's grave. They do not pay for my horses and cattle.*

Reader 3: *Good words do not give me back my children.*

Reader 4: *Good words will not make good* [your promises].

It Makes My Heart Sick:
Chief Joseph Speaks *(cont.)*

Part 3: Good Words and Broken Promises *(cont.)*

Reader 1: *Good words will not give my people a home where they can live in peace and take care of themselves. I am tired of talk that comes to nothing. It makes my heart sick when I remember all the good words and all the broken promises.*

Reader 2: *There has been too much talking by men who had no right to talk.*

Reader 3: *Too many misinterpretations have been made;*

Reader 4: *too many misunderstandings have come up between the white men and the Indians.*

Reader 1: *If the white man wants to live in peace with the Indian, he can live in peace. There need be no trouble. Treat all men alike. Give them the same laws. Give them all an even chance to live and grow.*

All men were made by the same Great Spirit Chief. They are all brothers.

Reader 2: *The earth is the mother of all people, and all people should have equal rights upon it . . . .*

Reader 3: *If you pen an Indian up on a small spot of earth and compel him to stay there, he will not be contented nor will he grow and prosper.*

Reader 4: *I have asked some of the Great White Chiefs where they get their authority to say to the Indian that he shall stay in one place, while he sees white men going where they please. They cannot tell me.*

Reader 1: *. . . When I think of our condition, my heart is heavy. I see men of my own race treated as outlaws and driven from country to country, or shot down like animals.*

#50113—Building Fluency through Practice and Performance © *Shell Education*

It Makes My Heart Sick:
Chief Joseph Speaks *(cont.)*

Part 3: Good Words and Broken Promises *(cont.)*

Reader 2: . . . *We only ask an even chance to live as other men live.*

Reader 3: *We ask that the same law shall work alike on all men.*

Reader 4: . . . *Let me be a free man,*

Reader 1: *free to travel,*

Reader 2: *free to stop,*

Reader 3: *free to work,*

Reader 4: *free to trade where I choose,*

Reader 1: *free to choose my own teachers,*

Reader 2: *free to follow the religion of my fathers,*

Reader 3: *free to talk, think and act for myself—*

Reader 4: *and I will obey every law or submit to the penalty.*

Reader 1: *Whenever the white man treats the Indian as they treat each other then we shall have no more wars.*

All: ***We shall be all alike—brothers of one father and mother, with one sky above us and one country around us and one government for all.***

Reader 2: *Then, the Great Spirit Chief who rules above will smile upon this land and send rain to wash out the bloody spots made by brothers' hands upon the face of the earth.*

Reader 3: *For this time, the Indian race is waiting and praying.*

It Makes My Heart Sick: Chief Joseph Speaks *(cont.)*

Part 3: Good Words and Broken Promises *(cont.)*

Reader 4:   *I hope no more groans of wounded men and women will ever go to the ear of the Great Spirit Chief above, and that all people may be one people.*

Reader 2:   *Hin-mah-too-lat-kekt has spoken for his people.*

Narrator: In 1885, Chief Joseph was sent along with many of his band to a reservation in Washington. According to the reservation doctor, he later died of a broken heart.

Extension Suggestion

After reading this, work with your partner to make a time line showing Chief Joseph's life and the trials of the Nez Percé.

Background Information

The Nez Percé lived on a large reservation in the Northwest. Then, white miners found gold on their land. The government wanted to make the reservation smaller. This way, land could be given to miners and settlers. Chief Joseph would not sign a new treaty. One day, some Nez Percé warriors attacked white settlers. The United States Army came to force the tribe to a smaller reservation. This is when the long battle began. After three months, Chief Joseph and his people were tired of fighting.

I Do Not Believe in Woman Suffrage: Based on the Writings of Marie Jenney Howe, 1913

Edited by Stephen Griffith; Arranged by Stephen and Lorraine Griffith

A reader's theater for three voices

R1: After more than 60 years of struggle, the women's suffrage campaigns finally began to reach wide audiences in 1910. This may have happened because suffragists learned how to spread their messages through imaginative use of various media. Suffragists used brief plays and monologues to enliven their own meetings and to enlist new members. One example of a 1913 creative argument is Marie Jenney Howe's *The Antisuffrage Monologue*. In it, she parodied anti-suffragist arguments that relied on stereotypes of female dependence, irrationality, and delicacy even as they also warned that women voters would exert too much power. Following are some excerpts:

R2: Please do not think of me as old-fashioned. I pride myself on being a modern up-to-date woman. I believe in all kinds of broad-mindedness, only I do not believe in woman suffrage because to do that would be to deny I'm a woman.

R3: Man must remain man. Woman must remain woman. If man goes over and tries to be like woman, if woman goes over and tries to be like man, it will become so very confusing and so difficult to explain to our children. Let us take a practical example. If a woman puts on a man's coat and trousers, takes a man's cane and hat and cigar, and goes out on the street, what will happen to her? She will be arrested and thrown into jail. Then why not stay at home?

R1: My argument against suffrage is that the women would not use it if they had it. You couldn't drive them to the polls. My second argument is, if the women were enfranchised they would neglect their homes, desert their families, and spend all their time at the polls. You may tell me that the polls are only open once a year. But I know women. They are creatures of habit. If you let them go to the polls once a year, they will hang round the polls all the rest of the time.

R2: If the women were enfranchised they would vote exactly as their husbands do and only double the existing vote. Do you like that argument? If not, take this one. If the women were enfranchised they would vote against their own husbands, thus creating dissension, family quarrels, and divorce.

I Do Not Believe in Woman Suffrage: Based on the Writings of Marie Jenney Howe, 1913 *(cont.)*

R3: My argument is—women are angels. Many men call me an angel and I have a strong instinct which tells me it is true; that is why I am anti, because "I want to be an angel and with the angels stand." And if you don't like that argument take this one. Women are depraved. They would introduce into politics a vicious element which would ruin our national life.

R1: And here is another issue—women cannot understand politics. Therefore there would be no use in giving women political power, because they would not know what to do with it. On the other hand, if the women were enfranchised, they would mount rapidly into power, take all the offices from all the men, and soon we would have women governors of all our states and dozens of women acting as President of the United States.

R2: And women cannot band together. They are incapable of organization. No two women can even be friends. Women are cats. On the other hand, if women were enfranchised, we would have all the women banded together on one side and all the men banded together on the other side, and there would follow a war which might end in revolution.

R3: Besides, the ballot is greatly over-estimated. It has never done anything for anybody. Lots of men tell me this. And the corresponding argument is—the ballot is what makes man, man. It is what gives him all his dignity and all of his superiority to women. Therefore if we allow women to share this privilege, how could a woman look up to her own husband? Why, there would be nothing to look up to.

R1: Now, I think I have proved anti-suffrage; and I have done it in a womanly way—that is, without stooping to the use of a single fact or argument or a single statistic.

R2: We antis do not believe that any conditions should be altered. We want everything to remain just as it is. All is for the best. Whatever is, is right. If misery is in the world, God has put it there; let it remain. If this misery presses harder on some women than others, it is because they need discipline. Now, I have always been comfortable and well cared for. But then I never needed discipline. Of course I am only a weak, ignorant woman. But there is one thing I do understand from the ground up, and that is the divine intention toward woman. I know that the divine intention toward woman is, let her remain at home.

I Do Not Believe in Woman Suffrage: Based on the Writings of Marie Jenney Howe, 1913 *(cont.)*

R3: It comes down to this. Someone must wash the dishes. Now, would you expect man, man made in the image of God, to roll up his sleeves and wash the dishes? Why, it would be blasphemy. I know that I am but a rib and so I wash the dishes. Or I hire another rib to do it for me, which amounts to the same thing.

R1: Have you envisioned Election Day with women voting? Imagine the pressure on the brain, the mental strain on woman's delicate nervous system and her highly wrought sensitive nature. Can you imagine how women, having undergone the terrible ordeal of voting, with their delicate systems all upset, will come out of the voting booths and be led away by policemen, and put into ambulances, while they are fainting and weeping, half laughing, half crying, and having fits upon the public highway? Don't you think that if a woman is going to have a fit, it is far better for her to have it in the privacy of her own home?

R2: And how shall I picture to you the terrors of the day after election? Divorce and death will rage unchecked, crime and contagious disease will stalk unbridled through the land.

R3: Oh, friends, on this subject I feel . . . I feel so strongly that I cannot think!

Background Information

The word *suffrage* means the right to vote. For many years, bills concerning women's suffrage were brought before Congress. In 1920, the Nineteenth Amendment to the United States Constitution was ratified and women were given the right to vote.

From Adversity to Success: The Jesse Owens Story

A reader's theater for five voices: four narrators and Jesse Owens

Owens: Didn't have much money. Worked many jobs. Struggled with segregation. KEEP IN MIND: The only victory that counts is the one over yourself.

Narrator 1: For a black family in the rural south, life was hard in the early 1900s. Everything in America was still segregated—schools, restaurants, hotels, trains, water fountains—everything. In the northern states, there was segregation, too; but doors were opening faster there for blacks. Jesse Owens was born in the segregated South to Emma and Henry Owens.

All Narrators: 1913

Narrator 2: My boy, James Cleveland Owens—we called him J.C.—was born in Alabama. We were poor sharecroppers. When J.C. was eight, we moved north to Cleveland, Ohio, where my husband hoped for a better job.

Narrator 1: On his first school day in Cleveland, when the teacher asked his name, she heard "Jesse" instead of J.C. After that he was always called Jesse.

Narrator 2: Jesse always liked to run.

Narrator 1: At Fairmount Junior High, Coach Charlie Riley recognized that the young Jesse was a talented runner.

Owens: Didn't have much money. Worked many jobs. Struggled with segregation. KEEP IN MIND: The only victory that counts is the one over yourself.

Narrator 4: Jesse and I met in junior high.

#50113—Building Fluency through Practice and Performance   © *Shell Education*

From Adversity to Success: The Jesse Owens Story *(cont.)*

All Narrators: **1927**

Narrator 3: Jesse couldn't practice after school. His family was poor, and he needed to work. So he trained with me in the mornings.

Owens: Every morning, just like in Alabama, I got up with the sun, ate my breakfast even before my mother and sisters and brothers, and went to school, winter, spring, and fall alike to run and jump and bend my body this way and that for Mr. Charles Riley.

Narrator 3: Jesse was strong by the time he got to East Technical High School. He tied the world record in the 100-yard dash and leaped 24 feet, 9 5/8 inches in the broad jump at a meet in Chicago. Jesse was recruited by Ohio State but wasn't even awarded a scholarship.

All Narrators: **1933**

Narrator 1: Jesse had to live off campus with other black athletes. When the team traveled, he had to eat at "blacks only" restaurants and sleep in "blacks only" hotels.

All Narrators: **1935**

Narrator 3: After falling down some stairs, Jesse was in a lot of pain for the Big Ten Meet in Ann Arbor, Michigan, but he wanted to compete. That day he tied the record for the 100-yard dash, shattered the world record for the broad jump, and set a new world record for the 220-yard dash. Then, he finished the day by setting a new world record in the 220-yard low hurdles.

Owens: Didn't have much money. Worked many jobs. Struggled with segregation. KEEP IN MIND: The only victory that counts is the one over yourself.

From Adversity to Success: The Jesse Owens Story *(cont.)*

All Narrators: **1935**

Narrator 4:   Jesse and I got married. We would later have three daughters, Gloria, Marlene, and Beverly. Jesse said what he loved most about me was that I didn't care that we were poor. I wasn't bothered by other peoples' prejudices. I never really cared what the world said or did. I had a voice inside me that said I was perfect.

Narrator 3:   By his sophomore year in college, Jesse and I both knew he could compete . . . at a higher level.

Owens: Coach was constantly on me about the job I was to do and the responsibility I had on the campus. I must be able to carry myself because people were looking.

All Narrators: **1936**

Narrator 1:   Jesse entered the 1936 Olympic Games in Berlin, Germany.

Narrator 2:   We were so nervous about Jesse going to those games. Hitler wanted to prove to the world that whites—he called them Aryans—were the supreme race. He didn't want people like Jesse showing up his athletes.

Owens: I wanted no part of politics. And I wasn't in Berlin to compete against any one athlete. The purpose of the Olympics, anyway, was to do your best. As I'd learned long ago from Coach Riley, the only victory that counts is the one over yourself.

Narrator 3:   Jesse won the 100-meter dash.

Owens: To a sprinter, the 100-meter dash is over in a second, not 9 or 10. It seems to take an eternity, yet all is over before you can think about what is happening.

#50113—Building Fluency through Practice and Performance   © *Shell Education*

From Adversity to Success:
The Jesse Owens Story *(cont.)*

Narrator 3:   Then, he won the 200-meter dash.

Owens: I fought, I fought harder.

Narrator 3:   And then, Jesse won the broad jump.

Owens: I decided I wasn't going to come down. I was going to fly. I was going to stay up in the air forever.

Narrator 3:   Then, Jesse ran on the 4 x 100-meter relay team and won again.

Owens: It dawned on me with blinding brightness. I had jumped into another rare kind of stratosphere—one that only a handful of people in every generation are lucky enough to know.

Narrator 3:   Four gold medals!

Owens: Didn't have much money. Worked many jobs. Struggled with segregation. KEEP IN MIND: The only victory that counts is the one over yourself.

Narrator 1:   If Jesse were around today, he would be a rich man after winning all those races. But in that time, there were no endorsements for a black man—no commercials, no print advertisements, no nothing.

Owens: After I came home from the 1936 Olympics with my four medals, it became increasingly apparent that everyone was going to slap me on the back, want to shake my hand, or have me up to their suite. But no one was going to offer me a job.

Narrator 2:   We were still poor. Jesse had to quit college and go to work.

Narrator 3:   What a shame for such a great athlete. To make money, Jesse would race anything or anybody—horses, motorcycles, major league ballplayers.

From Adversity to Success: The Jesse Owens Story *(cont.)*

Owens: It was bad enough to have toppled from the Olympic heights to make my living competing with animals. But the competition wasn't even fair. No man could beat a race horse, not even for 100 yards.

Narrator 2: My Jesse could always talk. He used that voice to speak to any group that would pay. He always remembered to talk about how important religion, hard work, and loyalty were.

Owens: Didn't have much money. Worked many jobs. Struggled with segregation. KEEP IN MIND: The only victory that counts is the one over yourself.

Narrator 3: Jesse never forgot how important sports were when he was a youth. So he sponsored and took part in many youth sports programs in neighborhoods just like the one where he grew up.

All Narrators: 1976

Narrator 1: President Gerald Ford awarded Jesse Owens the Medal of Freedom, the highest honor a U.S. citizen can receive. He overcame segregation, racism, and bigotry to prove to the world that African Americans belonged in the world of athletics.

Owens: Didn't have much money. Worked many jobs. Struggled with segregation. KEEP IN MIND: The only victory that counts is the one over yourself.

All Narrators: 1980

Narrator 4: My Jessie died on March 31, 1980. He fought his cancer until the very end—just like he fought in the world of athletics. Jesse, you worked—possibly *slaved* is the word—for many years. You deserve everything they're saying about you.

#50113—Building Fluency through Practice and Performance

From Adversity to Success:
The Jesse Owens Story *(cont.)*

Narrator 1: Jessie's wife and daughters continue his important work. They operate the Jesse Owens Foundation, which supports deserving young people who pursue their goals. Jesse would certainly be proud of their efforts.

Narrator 3: It all goes so fast. And character makes the difference when it's close.

Background Information

At the 1936 Olympics, Owens ran the 100-meter dash in 10.3 seconds. He ran the 200-meter dash in 20.7 seconds. His team took only 39.8 seconds to win the 4 x 100-meter relay. This particular Olympics was held in Nazi Germany just before the beginning of World War II. Back then, many did not believe that black people were as good as white people. Owens proved these people wrong.

Rosa Parks, December 1, 1955

Written by Curtis Treece

A reader's theater for five voices

Narrator 1: It had been a workday like most others for 42-year-old Rosa Parks.

Narrator 2: Mrs. Parks had spent the day at her job in the department store, bent over her sewing machine, making alterations on customers' new clothes.

Narrator 3: But now it was time to go home.

Narrator 1: What took place that night changed the United States forever. We know what happened, but we don't know exactly what was said. One could imagine the story unfolding as follows:

Rosa Parks: *(talking to herself)* My goodness, my feet and back sure do ache! I'd rather not have to ride that bus again, but I sure am tired! And it's over a mile walk home. I guess I'll just have to put up with the bus today.

Narrator 1: Mrs. Parks hated riding the buses. The "Jim Crow" laws in Montgomery, Alabama, and in many other places in the South made riding the buses a humiliating experience for black passengers like Mrs. Parks.

Narrator 2: First, a black bus rider had to go in the front door of the bus to pay the fare, then, get off the bus, and enter the back door to sit in the back of the bus with other black passengers.

Narrator 3: And, to make matters worse, black passengers had to move or even stand if a white person needed a seat . . . even though black and white passengers paid the same amount of money to ride!

Rosa Parks: *(still talking to herself)* I got here to the bus stop just in time. Here comes a bus now! *(pause)* Oh, no, not him again!

#50113—Building Fluency through Practice and Performance © *Shell Education*

Rosa Parks, December 1, 1955 *(cont.)*

Narrator 1: The bus came to a halt and the door opened. This bus driver, a white man, was one who Mrs. Parks remembered well.

Narrator 2: He was the same driver who, years earlier, had left Mrs. Parks at the bus stop after she had paid her fare and had gotten off the bus to enter at the back door. That happened quite often to black passengers.

Bus Driver: *(grouchily)* Well, come on lady. You gonna ride or are you gonna stand there on the curb daydreaming?

Rosa Parks: *(sighing)* I'll ride. Here's my money.

Bus Driver: Well, hurry it up. I haven't got all day to wait for you.

Narrator 3: Mrs. Parks entered the back door of the bus and looked around for a seat among the other black passengers.

Narrator 1: The closest empty seat was midway up the aisle, just behind the white passengers' section.

Narrator 2: She plopped down in that seat and closed her eyes for a while to ease the weariness of a day of hard work.

Narrator 3: As she relaxed, the bus made one stop after another, and the front section of the bus quickly filled with white passengers who were also heading home from their jobs.

Narrator 1: Then, at the next stop, a white man got on the bus. He looked around in the white section for an empty seat, and after finding none there, went to tell the bus driver.

Narrator 2: Rosa Parks knew what was coming next. And, she made a decision that would affect not just her future, but also the futures of black people throughout the United States.

Rosa Parks, December 1, 1955 *(cont.)*

Bus Driver: Hey, you!

Narrator 3:   Mrs. Parks knew the driver was talking to her, but she pretended not to notice.

Bus Driver: You . . . with the glasses! Get up. This man needs a seat.

Narrator 1:   Mrs. Parks looked out her window and didn't move.

Narrator 2:   The driver pulled up the brakes, and angrily stomped down the aisle.

Bus Driver: This man needs your seat. Get up. NOW!

Rosa Parks: *(calmly)* No.

Narrator 3:   The other passengers, white and black, looked on eagerly to see what would happen next. The driver's face was turning red with anger, but he seemed unsure about what to do next.

Bus Driver: I said to GET UP! MOVE IT! THAT'S the LAW!

Rosa Parks: *(still calm)* No. I won't move. I won't argue with you. I won't fight or fuss. But I won't move.

Bus Driver: Lady, you're in for BIG trouble! Get out of that seat right now, or I'm calling the police to GET you out!

Rosa Parks: If that's what you must do, do it. This is my seat. I'm tired and I deserve to keep my seat, law or no law.

Narrator 1:   The driver returned to the front of the bus to call the police on his radio. Many of the white passengers shot angry looks at Mrs. Parks for being the cause of the delay.

#50113—*Building Fluency through Practice and Performance*   © *Shell Education*

Rosa Parks, December 1, 1955 *(cont.)*

Narrator 2: Rosa Parks knew that she was about to be arrested. She decided that she would go to jail peacefully, with dignity.

Rosa Parks: *(to herself)* I am so very tired! True, my body is tired, but mostly my spirit is tired of these laws and roles. I'm tired of injustice. I'm tired of being treated unfairly. I'm tired of disrespect. I may go to jail for sitting down, but today I've stood up for fairness and justice.

Narrator 3: And because of Rosa Parks's brave decision, others in her community decided that it was time for them to take action as well. Her refusal and the bus boycott that followed ignited a fire inside thousands of Americans, black and white, to work together to change laws.

Background Information

Rosa Parks was a tired seamstress on this day in 1955. But, it is important to realize that she was also an active member of the local National Association for the Advancement of Colored People (NAACP). Her decision to not give up her seat was not made lightly. She knew the consequences. She also knew that someone needed to make a big step so that the country would be forced to change.

Excerpts from President John F. Kennedy's Civil Rights Address, June 13, 1963

Good evening, my fellow citizens:

This afternoon, following a series of threats and defiant statements, the presence of Alabama National Guardsmen was required on the University of Alabama to carry out the final and unequivocal order of the United States District Court of the Northern District of Alabama. That order called for the admission of two clearly qualified young Alabama residents who happened to have been born Negro. That they were admitted peacefully on the campus is due in good measure to the conduct of the students of the University of Alabama, who met their responsibilities in a constructive way.

This Nation was founded by men of many nations and backgrounds. It was founded on the principle that all men are created equal, and that the rights of every man are diminished when the rights of one man are threatened.

Today we are committed to a worldwide struggle to promote and protect the rights of all who wish to be free. And when Americans are sent to Vietnam or West Berlin, we do not ask for whites only. It ought to be possible, therefore, for American students of any color to attend any public institution they select without having to be backed up by troops. It ought to be possible for American consumers of any color to receive equal service in places of public accommodation, such as hotels and restaurants and theaters and retail stores, without being forced to resort to demonstrations in the street. It ought to be possible for American citizens of any color to register and to vote in a free election without interference or fear of reprisal. It ought to be possible, in short, for every American to enjoy the privileges of being American without regard to his race or his color. In short, every American ought to have the right to be treated as he would wish to be treated, as one would wish his children to be treated. But this is not the case today.

The heart of the question is whether all Americans are to be afforded equal rights and equal opportunities, whether we are going to treat our fellow Americans as we want to be treated. If an American, because his skin is dark, cannot eat lunch in a restaurant open to the public, if he cannot send his children to the best public school available, if he cannot vote for the public officials who will represent him, if, in short, he cannot enjoy the full and free life which all of us want, then who among us would be content to have the color of his skin changed and stand in his place? Who among us would then be content with the counsels of patience and delay?

Excerpts from President John F. Kennedy's Civil Rights Address, June 13, 1963 *(cont.)*

One hundred years of delay have passed since President Lincoln freed the slaves, yet their heirs, their grandsons, are not fully free. They are not yet freed from the bonds of injustice. They are not yet freed from social and economic oppression. And this nation, for all its hopes and all its boasts, will not be fully free until all its citizens are free.

We preach freedom around the world, and we mean it, and we cherish our freedom here at home; but are we to say to the world, and, much more importantly, to each other, that this is the land of the free except for the Negroes; that we have no second-class citizens except Negroes; that we have no class or caste system, no ghettoes, no master race, except with respect to Negroes?

Now the time has come for this Nation to fulfill its promise. The events in Birmingham and elsewhere have so increased the cries for equality that no city or state or legislative body can prudently choose to ignore them. The fires of frustration and discord are burning in every city, North and South, where legal remedies are not at hand. Redress is sought in the streets, in demonstrations, parades, and protests which create tensions and threaten violence and threaten lives.

We face, therefore, a moral crisis as a country and as a people. It cannot be met by repressive police action. It cannot be left to increased demonstrations in the streets. It cannot be quieted by token moves or talk. It is a time to act in the Congress, in your state and local legislative bodies and, above all, in all of our daily lives. It is not enough to pin the blame on others, to say this is a problem of one section of the country or another, or deplore the facts that we face. A great change is at hand, and our task, our obligation, is to make that revolution, that change, peaceful and constructive for all. Those who do nothing are inviting shame as well as violence. Those who act boldly are recognizing right as well as reality.

I am, therefore, asking the Congress to enact legislation giving all Americans the right to be served in facilities which are open to the public—hotels, restaurants, theaters, retail stores, and similar establishments. This seems to me to be an elementary right. Its denial is an arbitrary indignity that no American in 1963 should have to endure. But many do.

Excerpts from President John F. Kennedy's Civil Rights Address, June 13, 1963 *(cont.)*

I want to pay tribute to those citizens North and South, who have been working in their communities to make life better for all. They are acting not out of sense of legal duty but out of a sense of human decency. Like our soldiers and sailors in all parts of the world, they are meeting freedom's challenge on the firing line, and I salute them for their honor and their courage.

This is one country. It has become one country because all the people who came here had an equal chance to develop their talents. We cannot say to ten percent of the population that you can't have that right; that your children cannot have the chance to develop whatever talents they have; that the only way that they are going to get their rights is to go into the streets and demonstrate. I think we owe them and we owe ourselves a better country than that.

Therefore, I'm asking for your help in making it easier for us to move ahead and to provide the kind of equality of treatment which we would want ourselves; to give a chance for every child to be educated to the limit of his talents.

As I have said before, not every child has an equal talent or an equal ability or an equal motivation, but they should have the equal right to develop their talent and their ability and their motivation, to make something of themselves.

This is what we're talking about and this is a matter which concerns this country and what it stands for, and in meeting it I ask the support of all our citizens.

Thank you very much.

Background Information

With this speech, President John F. Kennedy committed the United States government to fulfilling the promise offered to African Americans with the Emancipation Proclamation 100 years before.

Voices from the Civil Rights Movement

Compiled by Wendy Conklin

William Minner

William Minner lived in Oklahoma. He remembers a story about getting water when he was a boy.

"We had stopped at a spring. It was a very popular place where both blacks and whites would go to get water. We had waited there for about 30 minutes. But the people ahead of us, they were all white. When we had reached our turn, two white men grabbed my dad. They told him that he'd have to wait until all of the white people were finished. Dad said, 'We'll get our water another day or we'll come back.' They wouldn't let my dad leave. They said, 'You're going to stay here, and when all of the good white people have gotten their water, and when everyone is gone, then you can do what you want to.' When all the white people finished getting their water, Dad got his water. I remember him telling me, 'What you saw there was real hatred and prejudice. But this is not going to be forever . . . there's gonna come a day when this won't be anymore.'"

Effie Jones Bowers

Effie Jones Bowers was a student at Hall High School in Little Rock, Arkansas. She helped desegregate this high school. This is a story of her first day there.

"That first day was a scary day. We were trying not to be afraid. We were talking, and I believe they had blocked some cars that had come by, and people were hollering at us, and the police were all out there, and we just knew that we were going to try to be strong. They told us to just go straight and don't look back . . . . you know, they just called us all kind of trash. So we kept going and we got to Hall and we went on up the steps and went in the school. When we got in the school that's where everybody was. They were all standing there in this hall. Then finally someone ushered us which way to go."

Voices from the Civil Rights Movement *(cont.)*

Frank McCain

Frank McCain was a student who participated in the 1960 sit-in at the whites only Woolworth lunch counter. He tells about his experience there.

"There was a little old white lady who was finishing up her coffee at the counter. She strode toward me and I said to myself, 'Oh my, someone to spit in my face or slap my face.' I was prepared for it. But she stands behind Joseph McNeil and me and puts her hands on our shoulders. She said, 'Boys, I'm so proud of you. I only regret that you didn't do this 10 years ago.'"

Sarah Rudolph

Sarah Rudolph was inside the 16th Street Baptist Church in Birmingham, Alabama, the day it was bombed. She lost her eye and her sister Addie that day.

"Addie was standing by the window. Denise McNair asked Addie to tie the sash on her dress. I started to look toward them just to see them, but by the time I went to turn my head that way there was a loud noise. I didn't know what it was. I called out Addie's name about three or four times, but she didn't answer. All of a sudden, I heard a man outside holler, 'Someone just bombed the 16th Street church.' He came in, picked me up in his arms, and carried me out of the church. They took me over to the hospital . . . The doctor told me after they operated on my face that I had about 22 shards of glass in my face. When it was all over with, they took the patches off my eye and I had lost my right eye, and I could barely see out of my left eye. I stayed in the hospital about two-and-a-half months."

Mary Frances Mayes

Mary Frances Mayes talks about white people not letting her vote. They made her answer questions to see if she was smart enough to cast her ballot.

"I didn't ever have any fear. I wanted to go vote, but I didn't have nobody to carry me because they was scared. And when I did go over there to vote, they asked me, 'How many grains of corn on a cob? How many seeds in a watermelon?' I said, 'How do you know unless you cut it open and count it?'"

#50113—Building Fluency through Practice and Performance

Voices from the Civil Rights Movement *(cont.)*

Harold Dahmer

The Ku Klux Klan bombed Harold Dahmer's house in 1966. He tells about how his brother saved his life.

"My brother Dennis came and woke me up. He told me the house was on fire and he got me out of there. The house was engulfed in flames. My father was covered with smoke and soot, skin was hanging off his arms. My aunt carried him to the hospital. We waited for the fire truck to get there; it took about 35 or 45 minutes to get there and it was just six miles away. Let's just put it this way, they weren't in any hurry to get there. I knew what we were doing about voter registration, but it never occurred to me that something like this would happen. We were just trying to help other people."

Background Information

The Civil Rights Movement in the United States has many voices. These voices are just a few of the thousands affected by the violence and segregation of this period in history.

Performance Suggestion

This is a reader's theater for a pair of students. Both students read the bold type. Then, one student reads the background information and the other student reads the quotation.

A Tribute To Dr. Martin Luther King Jr.

Adapted by Timothy Rasinski

A reader's theater for four voices

Narrator 1: A man of God, a great American, a martyr to the cause of justice, equality, and freedom. These are words that describe Martin Luther King Jr.

Narrator 2: He spoke of a dream in which all people, regardless of the color of their skin, or their religious beliefs, or their ethnic heritage, would be treated with fairness and with dignity.

Narrator 3: Sadly, during Dr. King's lifetime, justice, equality, and freedom were nothing more than dreams for many Americans.

Narrator 1: You see, during Dr. King's lifetime, black people in the United States were treated differently than white people.

Narrator 2: Black people could not eat in the same restaurants as whites in some states.

Narrator 3: Black children could not attend the same schools as white children.

Narrator 2: Black people could not even use the same restrooms or water fountains as white people.

Narrator 1: This was not fair. And around the country, black people and white people began to speak out against this unfairness.

Narrator 2: Dr. King was one of the leaders of those who, through their actions and their words, demanded that America live up to its promise of a land of opportunity for all people, blacks, whites, Asians, Hispanics, American Indians, and all others.

A Tribute To Dr. Martin Luther King Jr. *(cont.)*

King: *I have a dream that one day this nation will rise up and live out the true meaning of its creed . . . that all men are created equal.*

Narrator 1: In the summer of 1963, Dr. King spoke at a special gathering of people dedicated to civil rights and equal rights for all people. The meeting was held in Washington, D.C., in the front of the Lincoln Memorial and the statue of Abraham Lincoln, the president who ended slavery during the Civil War, 100 years earlier.

Narrator 2: And still, even 100 years after the end of slavery, black people were still treated as second-class citizens in most parts of the United States.

Narrator 1: Dr. King helped all Americans see that this was not right, that no American should be satisfied with a country that treats people differently just because some have black skin while others have white skin.

King: *I can never be satisfied as long as our children are stripped of their selfhood and robbed of their dignity . . .*

Narrator 2: But the road to justice is a long and hard road. Many people attending this assembly had already been hard at work trying to make things better for all people in America. Dr. King urged them to keep the faith and to continue their work.

King: *I have a dream . . .*

Narrator 3: Dr. King knew that the work of people of goodwill dedicated to liberty and justice for all would eventually lead to a new America, an America he saw in his dreams.

King: *So let freedom ring . . .*

Narrator 3: Dr. King was one of the greatest leaders of the Civil Rights Movement in the United States in the 1950s and 1960s.

A Tribute To Dr. Martin Luther King Jr. *(cont.)*

Narrator 1:   Unfortunately, he never lived to see the day when his dream of an America for all people became a reality.

Narrator 2:   In 1968, five years after giving his "I Have a Dream" speech, Dr. King traveled to Memphis, Tennessee, to support a strike by the city's sanitation workers. While standing on a balcony of a motel, Dr. King was shot and killed by an assassin.

Narrator 3:   Still the legacy of Dr. King lives on. The words and actions of Dr. King continue to inspire people today just at they did on that special day in 1963.

Narrator 1:   Dr. Martin Luther King Jr. taught us that people who want what is right, people who desire equality, justice, and freedom can make it happen by working for it. We continue to work for it today, so that one day all of us, no matter who we are or what we may look like, will be able to say,

King: *Free at last, free at last. Thank God Almighty, we are free at last!*

Background Information

Martin Luther King's "I Have a Dream" speech was delivered in 1963 in Washington, D.C. Many credit this speech with pushing leaders to create the Civil Rights Act of 1964. That year, King was awarded the Nobel Peace Prize. He was only 35 years old and the youngest man to have ever received that award. (You can find the full text of the speech online.)

Excerpts of Remarks by Robert F. Kennedy on the Day of the Assassination of Dr. Martin Luther King Jr.

Ladies and Gentlemen: I'm only going to talk to you just for a minute or so this evening. Because . . . I have some very sad news for all of you, and I think, sad news for all of our fellow citizens, and people who love people all over the world; and that is that Martin Luther King was shot and was killed tonight in Memphis, Tennessee.

Martin Luther King dedicated his life to love and to justice for his fellow human beings, and he died because of that effort. In this difficult day, in this difficult time for the United States, it's perhaps well to ask what kind of a nation we are and what direction we want to move in. For those of you who are black—considering the evidence there evidently is that there were white people who were responsible—you can be filled with bitterness, and with hatred, and a desire for revenge. We can move in that direction as a country, in great polarization—black people amongst blacks, and white people amongst whites, filled with hatred toward one another.

Or we can make an effort, as Martin Luther King did, to understand and to comprehend, and to replace that violence, that stain of bloodshed that has spread across our land, with an effort to understand, compassion and love.

For those of you who are black and are tempted to be filled with hatred and distrust of the injustice of such an act, against all white people, I can only say that I feel in my own heart the same kind of feeling. I had a member of my family killed, but he was killed by a white man. But we have to make an effort in the United States, we have to make an effort to understand, to get beyond, or go beyond these rather difficult times.

What we need in the United States is not division; what we need in the United States is not hatred; what we need in the United States is not violence and lawlessness but love and wisdom, and compassion toward one another, and a feeling of justice towards those who still suffer within our country, whether they be white or they be black.

So I shall ask you tonight to return home, to say a prayer for the family of Martin Luther King, that's true, but more importantly to say a prayer for our own country, which all of us love—a prayer for understanding and that compassion of which I spoke.

Excerpts of Remarks by Robert F. Kennedy on the Day of the Assassination of Dr. Martin Luther King *(cont.)*

We can do well in this country. We will have difficult times. We've had difficult times in the past. And we will have difficult times in the future. It is not the end of violence; it is not the end of lawlessness; it is not the end of disorder.

But the vast majority of white people and the vast majority of black people in this country want to live together, want to improve the quality of our life, and want justice for all human beings that abide in our land.

Let us dedicate ourselves to what the Greeks wrote so many years ago: to tame the savageness of man and to make gentle the life of this world.

Let us dedicate ourselves to that, and say a prayer for our country and for our people.

Thank you very much.

Background Information

Robert Kennedy was the brother of President John F. Kennedy. Robert Kennedy gave this speech to a group of African Americans in Indianapolis, Indiana. Originally, he was there to talk about his plans for running for president. He had just heard the news and could tell that the crowd did not know. Instead of campaigning for president, he broke the news to the crowd.

Modern Times

The Inauguration of President John Fitzgerald Kennedy

Written/Arranged by Lorraine Griffith

A reader's theater for six voices

R1: It was a chilly, but beautiful, snowy morning on January 20, 1961, when John Fitzgerald Kennedy was inaugurated as the 35th president of the United States of America. An inaugural ceremony is a defining moment in a president's career. After all of the campaign rhetoric, the president must summarize his hopes for his presidency.

R2: There are also expectations of great speechmaking. In fact, there are lines from presidential inaugural addresses that are part of our nation's culture now. Like Abraham Lincoln's second inaugural address presented to a hurting and divided nation, *"With malice toward none, with charity for all . . . "* Or like this one from Franklin D. Roosevelt during the depths of the Depression, *"The only thing we have to fear is fear itself."*

R3: As JFK prepared for his inaugural address, he had plenty of advisors, friends, and clergy available to help him write the speech. But he chose to study famous American speeches like the Gettysburg Address. After Kennedy wrote his speech by longhand on a long yellow legal pad, he revised every sentence countless times . . . until he had reduced his ideas to a relatively short inaugural speech with a bold message, devoting most of his speech to foreign affairs.

R4: And speaking of foreign affairs, there was a growing tension in 1961. There were already at least 900 American military advisors in Vietnam. Castro had seized power in Cuba the year before and just a few weeks before this inauguration day, the United States had cut off all diplomatic relations with Cuba. The Peace Corps hadn't been born yet. The Berlin Wall would be built soon.

R5: In this speech, Kennedy felt that he needed to set aside the political partisanship that heightens during every election and bring a message of unity in light of America's relationship with the world.

#50113—Building Fluency through Practice and Performance   © *Shell Education*

The Inauguration of President John Fitzgerald Kennedy *(cont.)*

R6: Little did he know that he too would join Lincoln and Roosevelt, presenting the American people with a phrase that would be forever woven into the fabric of our American history and culture.

All: *"And so, my fellow Americans: ask not what your country can do for you—ask what you can do for your country."*

R1–R2: Listen as we share the reading of this now famous speech,

R3–R4: first delivered in 1961,

R5–R6: on the steps of the Capitol that cold January day.

All: **President John F. Kennedy's Inaugural Address, 1961**

R1: *Vice President Johnson,*

R2: *Mr. Speaker, Mr. Chief Justice,*

R3: *President Eisenhower, Vice President Nixon,*

R4: *President Truman,*

R5: *Reverend Clergy,*

R6: *fellow citizens:*

R1: *We observe today not a victory of party but a celebration of freedom—symbolizing an end as well as a beginning—signifying renewal as well as change. For I have sworn before you and Almighty God the same solemn oath our forbears prescribed nearly a century and three-quarters ago.*

R2: *The world is very different now. For man holds in his mortal hands the power to abolish all forms of human poverty and all forms of human life. And yet the same revolutionary beliefs for which our forebears fought are still at issue around the globe—the belief that the rights of man come not from the generosity of the state but from the hand of God.*

The Inauguration of President John Fitzgerald Kennedy *(cont.)*

R3: *We dare not forget today that we are the heirs of that first revolution. Let the word go forth from this time and place, to friend and foe alike, that the torch has been passed to a new generation of Americans—born in this century, tempered by war, disciplined by a hard and bitter peace, proud of our ancient heritage—and unwilling to witness or permit the slow undoing of those human rights to which this nation has always been committed, and to which we are committed today at home and around the world.*

R4: *Let every nation know, whether it wishes us well or ill,*

R5: *that we shall pay any price,*

R6: *bear any burden,*

R5: *meet any hardship,*

R6: *support any friend,*

R4: *oppose any foe to assure the survival and the success of liberty.*

All: ***This much we pledge—and more.***

R1: *To those old allies whose cultural and spiritual origins we share, we pledge the loyalty of faithful friends. United there is little we cannot do in a host of cooperative ventures. Divided there is little we can do—for we dare not meet a powerful challenge at odds and split asunder.*

R2: *To those new states whom we welcome to the ranks of the free, we pledge our word that one form of colonial control shall not have passed away merely to be replaced by a far more iron tyranny. We shall not always expect to find them supporting our view. But we shall always hope to find them strongly supporting their own freedom—and to remember that, in the past, those who foolishly sought power by riding the back of the tiger ended up inside.*

#50113—Building Fluency through Practice and Performance © Shell Education

The Inauguration of President John Fitzgerald Kennedy *(cont.)*

R3: *To those people in the huts and villages of half the globe struggling to break the bonds of mass misery, we pledge our best efforts to help them help themselves, for whatever period is required—not because the communists may be doing it, not because we seek their votes, but because it is right. If a free society cannot help the many who are poor, it cannot save the few who are rich.*

R4: *To our sister republics south of our border, we offer a special pledge—to convert our good words into good deeds—in a new alliance for progress—to assist free men and free governments in casting off the chains of poverty. But this peaceful revolution of hope cannot become the prey of hostile powers. Let all our neighbors know that we shall join with them to oppose aggression or subversion anywhere in the Americas. And let every other power know that this Hemisphere intends to remain the master of its own house.*

R5: *To that world assembly of sovereign states, the United Nations, our last best hope in an age where the instruments of war have far outpaced the instruments of peace, we renew our pledge of support—to prevent it from becoming merely a forum for invective—to strengthen its shield of the new and the weak—and to enlarge the area in which its writ may run.*

R6: *Finally, to those nations who would make themselves our adversary, we offer not a pledge but a request: that both sides begin anew the quest for peace, before the dark powers of destruction unleashed by science engulf all humanity in planned or accidental self-destruction.*

R1: *We dare not tempt them with weakness. For only when our arms are sufficient beyond doubt can we be certain beyond doubt that they will never be employed.*

R2: *But neither can two great and powerful groups of nations take comfort from our present course—both sides overburdened by the cost of modern weapons, both rightly alarmed by the steady spread of the deadly atom, yet both racing to alter that uncertain balance of terror that stays the hand of mankind's final war.*

The Inauguration of President John Fitzgerald Kennedy *(cont.)*

All: *So let us begin anew—*

R3: *remembering on both sides that civility is not a sign of weakness, and sincerity is always subject to proof. Let us never negotiate out of fear. But let us never fear to negotiate.*

R4: *Let both sides explore what problems unite us instead of belaboring those problems which divide us.*

R5: *Let both sides, for the first time, formulate serious and precise proposals for the inspection and control of arms—and bring the absolute power to destroy other nations under the absolute control of all nations.*

R6: *Let both sides seek to invoke the wonders of science instead of its terrors. Together let us explore the stars, conquer the deserts, eradicate disease, tap the ocean depths and encourage the arts and commerce.*

R5: *Let both sides unite to heed in all corners of the earth the command of Isaiah— to "undo the heavy burdens . . . (and) let the oppressed go free."*

R4: *And if a beachhead of cooperation may push back the jungle of suspicion, let both sides join in creating a new endeavor, not a new balance of power, but a new world of law, where the strong are just and the weak secure and the peace preserved.*

R3: *All this will not be finished in the first one hundred days.*

R2: *Nor will it be finished in the first one thousand days,*

R1: *nor in the life of this Administration,*

R6: *nor even perhaps in our lifetime on this planet.*

All: *But let us begin.*

The Inauguration of President John Fitzgerald Kennedy *(cont.)*

R6:   *In your hands, my fellow citizens, more than mine, will rest the final success or failure of our course. Since this country was founded, each generation of Americans has been summoned to give testimony to its national loyalty. The graves of young Americans who answered the call to service surround the globe.*

R4–R5:   *Now the trumpet summons us again—*

R4:   *not as a call to bear arms, though arms we need—*

R5:   *not as a call to battle, though embattled we are—*

R4:   *but a call to bear the burden of a long twilight struggle, year in and year out, "rejoicing in hope, patient in tribulation"*

R5:   *—a struggle against the common enemies of man: tyranny, poverty, disease and war itself.*

R1:   *Can we forge against these enemies a grand and global alliance, North and South, East and West, that can assure a more fruitful life for all mankind? Will you join in that historic effort?*

R2:   *In the long history of the world, only a few generations have been granted the role of defending freedom in its hour of maximum danger. I do not shrink from this responsibility—I welcome it. I do not believe that any of us would exchange places with any other people or any other generation. The energy, the faith, the devotion which we bring to this endeavor will light our country and all who serve it—and the glow from that fire can truly light the world.*

All: ***And so, my fellow Americans: ask not what your country can do for you— ask what you can do for your country.***

R1–R2:   *My fellow citizens of the world: ask not what America will do for you, but what together we can do for the freedom of man.*

The Inauguration of President John Fitzgerald Kennedy *(cont.)*

R3: *Finally, whether you are citizens of America or citizens of the world,*

R4: *ask of us here the same high standards of strength and sacrifice which we ask of you.*

R5: *With a good conscience our only sure reward,*

R6: *with history the final judge of our deeds,*

All: ***let us go forth to lead the land we love,***

R2: *asking His blessing and His help,*

R3: *but knowing that here on earth God's work must truly be our own.*

Background Information

The day before President John Kennedy's inaugural address, it had snowed. Some thought that the celebration should be postponed because it was so cold, but Kennedy was eager to give his speech and rally the American public behind him. The ceremony went on as planned. You can find a recording of this text on the Internet if you want to hear Kennedy say it.

The Assassination of John Fitzgerald Kennedy: A Nation Bereaved

Edited by Stephen Griffith; Arranged by Stephen and Lorraine Griffith

A reader's theater for seven voices

Narrator 1: On November 24, 1963, in the rotunda of the United States Capitol, Earl Warren, Chief Justice of the Supreme Court, made the following remarks:

Earl Warren: *There are few events in our national life that unite Americans and so touch the hearts of all of us as the passing of a president of the United States.*

Narrator 2: At 1:40 P.M. Eastern Standard Time on November 22, 1963, the top-rated American soap opera "As the World Turns," was interrupted mid-scene by Walter Cronkite's voice delivering the following news flash:

Newsperson 1: *"Here is a bulletin from CBS News. In Dallas, Texas, three shots were fired on President Kennedy's motorcade in downtown Dallas. The first reports say that President Kennedy has been seriously wounded by this shooting . . . More details just arrived. These details about the same as previously. President Kennedy shot today just as his motorcade left downtown Dallas. Mrs. Kennedy jumped up and grabbed Mr. Kennedy. She called, 'Oh, no' and the motorcade sped on. United Press says that the wounds for President Kennedy perhaps could be fatal. Repeating, a bulletin from CBS News, President Kennedy has been shot by a would-be assassin in Dallas, Texas. Stay tuned to CBS News for further details."*

Narrator 2: "As the World Turns" continued for one more scene before Cronkite cut in —beginning 53 hours of nonstop reporting by CBS (and the other networks). The television coverage of the assassination was the longest uninterrupted news coverage of one event until the terrorist attacks on the World Trade Center and the Pentagon.

Earl Warren: *There is nothing that adds shock to our sadness as the assassination of our leader, chosen as he is to embody the ideals of our people, the faith we have in our institutions, and our belief in the fatherhood of God and the brotherhood of man.*

The Assassination of John Fitzgerald Kennedy: A Nation Bereaved *(cont.)*

Narrator 2: At 2:37 P.M. on November 22, CBS news editor Ed Bliss Jr. handed Cronkite an AP wire report. Cronkite, wearing black glasses, rolled-up white shirt sleeves, loosened tie, and no makeup, takes a moment to read it to himself before intoning:

Newsperson 1: *"From Dallas, Texas, this flash, apparently official. President Kennedy died at 1:00 P.M. Central Standard Time, two o'clock Eastern Standard Time."*

Narrator 2: He paused, as if disbelieving the words he had just said. He momentarily lost his composure, winced, removed his eyeglasses, and raised a hand to wipe away a tear before resuming with the news that President Kennedy had died while undergoing emergency surgery at Parkland Hospital.

Earl Warren: *Such misfortunes have befallen the Nation on other occasions,*

Narrator 2: Abraham Lincoln in 1865, James Garfield in 1881, and William McKinley in 1901

Earl Warren: *But never more shockingly than two days ago. We are saddened; we are stunned; we are perplexed.*

Narrator 1: The first hour after the shooting, before Kennedy's death was announced, was a time of great confusion. People began to huddle around radios and TVs for the latest bulletins. In cities around the world, people wept openly. People clustered in department stores to catch TV coverage, and others prayed. Motor traffic in some areas came to a halt as the news of Kennedy's death spread from car to car. Schools across the United States of America and Canada dismissed students early.

Earl Warren: *John Fitzgerald Kennedy, a great and good president, the friend of all men of good will, a believer in the dignity and equality of all human beings, a fighter for justice, an apostle of peace, has been snatched from our midst by the bullet of an assassin.*

The Assassination of John Fitzgerald Kennedy: A Nation Bereaved *(cont.)*

Narrator 4: The motorcade was to follow a winding 11-mile route through downtown Dallas, Texas. President Kennedy was to speak at a luncheon with civic and business leaders. At 11:50 A.M., the motorcade left the airport.

Narrator 5: The big presidential limousine, a midnight blue 1961 Lincoln, had been flown in from Washington, D.C. The plastic bubble top was removed and the bulletproof side windows were rolled down because the weather was so favorable, and this was how President Kennedy preferred to ride.

Narrator 4: The Secret Service's 1955 Cadillac convertible followed closely behind the president's limousine. It carried eight agents, with four posted on the running boards to quickly dismount the car to protect the president from the enthusiastic crowds.

Narrator 5: President and Mrs. Kennedy were in the back seat of the limousine while Texas Governor and Mrs. John Connolly were in the seats up front. The motorcade arrived in Dealey Plaza and then turned right from Main to Houston Street. Just seconds later, it took the 120-degree turn into Elm Street passing the School Book Depository Building. The crowds were larger than expected and very enthusiastic about the young president and his pretty wife.

Narrator 4: A shot rang out at 12:30 P.M. Central Standard Time. Kennedy's hands began to rise and he started to turn toward his wife. His expression had changed from a smile to astonishment.

Narrator 5: Riding in the front of the car, Secret Service agent Roy Kellerman said to the driver, Agent William Greer, "Let's get out of here." But the reaction was too slow for a bullet that can travel at 1,300 miles an hour.

President Kennedy was shot. The bullet exited through his neck. Kennedy got his hands up to neck and began to lean toward his wife.

Governor Connolly was also shot. He was shot through his back, his raised right hand, and his left thigh.

The Assassination of John Fitzgerald Kennedy: A Nation Bereaved *(cont.)*

Narrator 4: Agent Kellerman yelled, "We are hit." In the follow-up car, Agent George Hickey searched for a target but found none while Agent Clint Hill jumped from the running board of the car and moved toward the president.

With Jackie Kennedy looking on, a second shot entered the right side of President Kennedy's head. A huge mist of matter and blood spewed forth, covering everything nearby, including Mrs. Kennedy.

Narrator 5: Jackie Kennedy crawled onto the trunk of the limo. Agent Hill said he believed she was reaching for something coming off the right rear bumper of the car. Agent Hill managed to get onto the trunk and shove her back into the car. He placed his body over hers and the president's.

The limo now sped up to 80 miles an hour in a race to Parkland Hospital, which was four miles away.

Earl Warren: *What moved some misguided wretch to do this horrible deed may never be known to us.*

Narrator 1: The 1964 Warren Commission report on the John F. Kennedy assassination concluded that at 12:30 P.M. on November 22, 1963, Lee Harvey Oswald shot Kennedy from a window on the sixth floor of the Texas School Book Depository as the president's motorcade passed through Dealey Plaza.

Narrator 2: Immediately after he shot President Kennedy, Oswald hid the rifle behind some boxes and descended the Depository's rear staircase. On the second floor, he encountered Dallas police officer Marion Baker who had driven his motorcycle to the door of the Depository and sprinted up the stairs in search of the shooter. With him was Oswald's supervisor, Roy Truly, who identified Oswald as an employee. This caused Baker, who had his pistol in hand, to let Oswald pass. Oswald bought a Coke from a vending machine in the second floor lunchroom, crossed the floor to the front staircase, descended and left the building through the front entrance on Elm Street.

The Assassination of John Fitzgerald Kennedy: A Nation Bereaved *(cont.)*

Narrator 1: At about 12:40 P.M., Oswald boarded a city bus by pounding on the door in the middle of a block. When heavy traffic slowed the bus to a halt, he requested a bus transfer from the driver. He took a taxicab a few blocks beyond his rooming house at 1026 North Beckley Avenue. He then walked home to retrieve his revolver and beige jacket. This was about 1:00 P.M. Moments later he left the house. He lingered briefly at a bus stop across the street from his rooming house, then began walking.

Narrator 2: Officer J.D. Tippit had heard the general description of the alleged shooter, which was broadcast over the police radio at 12:45 P.M. Thirty minutes later, Tippit encountered Oswald near the corner of Patton Avenue and 10th Street and pulled up to talk to him through his patrol car window. Tippit got out of his car and Oswald fired at the police officer with his .38 caliber revolver. Four of the shots hit Tippit, killing him instantly in view of several witnesses. Oswald reloaded his revolver as he walked away, throwing the empty shell casings into some bushes. He then broke into a run, still holding the pistol in his hand.

Narrator 1: A few minutes later, Oswald ducked into the entrance alcove of a shoe store on Jefferson Street to avoid passing police cars. Then, he sneaked into the nearby Texas Theater. The shoe store's manager saw all of this, followed him, and alerted the theater's ticket clerk, who phoned police. Once inside, Oswald changed seats several times. The police quickly arrived and poured into the theater as the lights were turned on. Officer M.N. McDonald approached Oswald who was sitting near the rear and ordered him to stand.

Narrator 1: Oswald punched McDonald and drew his revolver. McDonald briefly struggled with Oswald before other officers subdued and arrested him at 1:50 P.M.

Narrator 2: Oswald was booked as a suspect in the shooting of Officer Tippit and shortly afterward on suspicion of murdering President Kennedy. By the end of the evening, he had been arraigned for both murders.

The Assassination of John Fitzgerald Kennedy: A Nation Bereaved *(cont.)*

Narrator 1: By the morning of Sunday, November 24, the Dallas police had already received many death threats directed towards Oswald. A homicide detective tried to convince the police captain to break his promise to reporters that they could photograph the suspected assassin as he was transferred to a nearby jail. The captain refused. Extensive precautions were taken to secure the area where Oswald would be briefly exposed to reporters and cameras.

Narrator 2: At 11:21 A.M. Central Standard Time, Oswald was shot and fatally wounded before live television cameras in the basement of Dallas police headquarters. Jack Ruby, a Dallas nightclub owner, committed the crime. This was the first time a homicide was captured and shown on live television. Later that day, Earl Warren delivered this message.

Earl Warren: *But we do know that such acts are commonly stimulated by forces of hatred and malevolence* [and] *. . . are eating their way into the bloodstream of American life. What a price we pay for this fanaticism.*

Narrator 3: In the history of the United States, nine American presidents—Andrew Jackson in 1835, Abraham Lincoln in 1865, James Garfield in 1881, William McKinley in 1901, Harry S. Truman in 1950, John F. Kennedy in 1963, Richard Nixon in 1974, Gerald Ford twice in 1975, and Ronald Reagan in 1981—have been the targets of assassination attempts. Attempts have also been made on the lives of one president-elect (Franklin D. Roosevelt in 1933) and two presidential candidates (Theodore Roosevelt in 1912 and George Wallace in 1972). In 1968, Robert F. Kennedy was assassinated as he ran for president. In addition, eight governors, seven U.S. senators, nine U.S. congressmen, eleven mayors, seventeen state legislators, and eleven judges have been violently attacked.

Earl Warren: *It has been said that the only thing we learn from history is that we do not learn. But surely we can learn, if we have the will to do so. Surely there is a lesson to be learned from this tragic event.*

Narrator 3: But do we learn? Since Kennedy's assassination, there continue to be ideological and political assassinations in the United States and around the world.

The Assassination of John Fitzgerald Kennedy: A Nation Bereaved *(cont.)*

Earl Warren: *If we really love this country, if we truly love justice and mercy, if we fervently want to make this Nation better for those who are to follow us, we can at least abjure [or reject] the hatred that consumes people, the false accusations that divide us, and the bitterness that begets violence. Is it too much to hope that the martyrdom of our beloved president might even soften the hearts of those who would themselves recoil from assassination, but who do not shrink from spreading the venom which kindles thoughts of it in others?*

Our Nation is bereaved. The whole world is poorer because of his loss. But we can all be better Americans because John Fitzgerald Kennedy has passed our way, because he has been our chosen leader at a time in history when his character, his vision, and his quiet courage have enabled him to chart for us a safe course through the shoals of treacherous seas that encompass the world.

Narrator 1: Did we miss our chance? Is the world a better place? Did we learn our lessons? I think not.

Earl Warren: *And now that he is relieved of the almost superhuman burdens we imposed on him, may he rest in peace.*

Extension Suggestion

After reading this piece, talk about the meaning behind this eulogy. Are there words that you need to define so that you understand it better? Now that you have discussed the meaning of the text, it should be more powerful when you read it. Your understanding will come through in your voice as you read more fluently.

Background Information

This script is based on a eulogy by Chief Justice Earl Warren and various news reports from November 22–24, 1963. Justice Warren was asked by Mrs. Kennedy to deliver this eulogy in the rotunda at the Capitol in a special ceremony.

Landing on the Moon

Written by Wendy Conklin

A reader's theater for three voices

Aldrin: Okay, everything's nice and sunny in here.

Armstrong: Okay, can you pull the door open a little more?

Aldrin: Did you get the mesa out?

Armstrong: I'm going to pull it now. Houston, the mesa came down all right.

Capcom: Houston. Roger, we copy, and we're standing by for your TV.

Armstrong: Houston, this is Neil. Radio check.

Capcom: Neil, this is Houston. You're loud and clear. Buzz, this is Houston. Radio check and verify TV circuit breaker in.

Aldrin: Roger, TV circuit breaker's in. Receive loud and clear.

Capcom: Man, we're getting a picture on the TV.

Aldrin: Oh, you got a good picture. Huh?

Capcom: There's a great deal of contrast in it, and currently it's upside-down on our monitor, but we can make out a fair amount of detail.

Aldrin: Okay, will you verify the position, the opening I ought to have on the camera.

Capcom: Okay, Neil, we can see you coming down the ladder now.

Armstrong: Okay, I just checked—getting back up to that first step, Buzz, it's not even collapsed too far, but it's adequate to get back up. It takes a pretty good little jump. I'm at the foot of the ladder. The Lunar Module footpads are only depressed in the surface about one or two inches. Although the surface appears to be very, very fine grained, as you get close to it. It's almost like a powder. Now and then, it's very fine. I'm going to step off the Lunar Module now . . . .

That's one small step for a man. One giant leap for mankind.

Landing on the Moon *(cont.)*

Armstrong: The surface is fine and powdery. I can pick it up loosely, with my toe. It does adhere in fine layers like powdered charcoal to the sole and sides of my boots. I only go in a small fraction of an inch. Maybe an eighth of an inch, but I can see the footprints of my boots and the treads in the fine sandy particles.

Capcom: Neil, this is Houston. We're copying.

Armstrong: There seems to be no difficulty in moving around as we suspected. It's even perhaps easier than the simulations that we performed on the ground. It's actually no trouble to walk around. The descent engine did not leave a crater of any size. There's about one foot clearance on the ground. We're essentially on a very level place here. I can see some evidence of rays emanating from the descent engine, but very insignificant amount. Okay, Buzz, we're ready to bring down the camera.

Aldrin: I'm all ready. I think it's been all squared away and in good shape. It looks like it's coming out nice and evenly.

Armstrong: Okay, it's quite dark here in the shadow and a little hard for me to see if I have good footing. I'll work my way over into the sunlight here without looking directly into the sun. Looking up at the Lunar Module, I'm standing directly in the shadow now looking up at Buzz in the window. And I can see everything quite clearly. The light is sufficiently bright, backlighted into the front of the Lunar Module, that everything is very clearly visible.

Armstrong: I'll step out and take some of my first pictures here.

Capcom: Roger, Neil, we're reading you loud and clear. We see you getting some pictures and the contingency sample.

Aldrin: He's getting some pictures and the contingency sample.

Armstrong: Rog, I'm going to get to that just as soon as I finish this picture series.

Aldrin: Okay the contingency sample is down. Looks like it's a little difficult to dig through.

Landing on the Moon *(cont.)*

Armstrong: This is very interesting. It's a very soft surface but here and there where I plug with the contingency sample collector, I run into a very hard surface but it appears to be very cohesive material of the same sort. I'll try to get a rock in here. Here's a couple.

Aldrin: That looks beautiful from here, Neil.

Armstrong: It has a stark beauty all its own. It's like much of the high desert of the United States. It's different but it's very pretty out here. Be advised that a lot of the rock samples out here, the hard rock samples have what appear to be vesicles in the surface. Also, I am looking at one now that appears to have some sort of phenocryst.

Armstrong: You can really throw things a long way out there.

Aldrin: Okay. I have got the cameras on at one frame a second.

Armstrong: Are you getting a TV picture now, Houston?

Capcom: Neil, yes, we are getting a TV picture. Neil, this is Houston. We're getting a picture here . . . . Here you come into our field of view.

Aldrin: Roger.

Armstrong: Hold it a second. First let me move that over the edge for you.

Aldrin: Okay. Are you ready for me to come out?

Armstrong: Yes. Just stand by a second. I'll move this over the handrail. Okay?

Aldrin: Alright. That's got it. Are you ready? Alright. The backup camera is in position . . . .

Armstrong: Looks good.

Aldrin: Now, I want to back up and partially close the hatch, making sure not to lock it on my way out.

Armstrong: A good thought.

Landing on the Moon *(cont.)*

Aldrin: That's our home for the next couple of hours and I want to take good care of it. Okay, I'm on the top step and I can look down over the landing gear pads. That's a very simple matter to hop down from one step to the next.

Armstrong: Yes, I found it to be very comfortable and walking is also very comfortable. You've got three more steps and then a long one.

Aldrin: Okay, I'm going to leave that one foot up there and both hands down to about the fourth rung up.

Armstrong: There you go. A little more. About another inch. There, you got it. That's a good step. About a three footer.

Aldrin: Beautiful, beautiful.

Armstrong: Isn't that something. Magnificent sight down here.

Background Information

On July 20, 1969, Neil Armstrong and Buzz Aldrin landed a Lunar Module on the moon. They spent 21 hours exploring the moon's surface and gathering rocks. This historic event was captured on camera and shown on television. This script is based on the transcript of the actual landing.

The Space Shuttle *Challenger*: A Speech Delivered by Ronald Reagan

Arranged by Lorraine Griffith

A reader's theater for six voices: two narrators (N) and four Reagans (R)

N1: It was January 28, 1986.

N2: Everyone had expected the president of the United States to deliver his annual State of the Union address.

N1: Instead of sharing his plans for the year ahead, he had to speak to the nation about a terrible tragedy that happened that same morning.

N2: A tragedy that involved space travel and school children . . . .

N1: Although one man spoke that night, four readers will share his now famous speech with you.

N2: Ronald Reagan was president and this is "The Space Shuttle *Challenger* Tragedy Address."

R1: *Ladies and Gentlemen, I'd planned to speak to you tonight to report on the state of the Union, but the events of earlier today have led me to change those plans. Today is a day for mourning and remembering. Nancy and I are pained to the core by the tragedy of the shuttle* Challenger. *We know we share this pain with all of the people of our country. This is truly a national loss.*

R2: *Nineteen years ago, almost to the day, we lost three astronauts in a terrible accident on the ground. But we've never lost an astronaut in flight. We've never had a tragedy like this. And perhaps we've forgotten the courage it took for the crew of the shuttle. But they, the "Challenger Seven" were aware of the dangers, but overcame them and did their jobs brilliantly. We mourn seven heroes:*

R3: *Michael Smith, Dick Scobee,*

R4: *Judith Resnik, Ronald McNair, Ellison Onizuka,*

R1: *Gregory Jarvis, and Christa McAuliffe.*

The Space Shuttle *Challenger*: A Speech Delivered by Ronald Reagan *(cont.)*

All: *We mourn their loss as a nation together.*

R2: *For the families of the seven, we cannot bear, as you do, the full impact of this tragedy. But we feel the loss, and we're thinking about you so very much.*

R3: *Your loved ones were daring and brave,*

R4: *and they had that special grace,*

R1: *that special spirit that says,*

All: *"Give me a challenge, and I'll meet it with joy."*

R2: *They had a hunger to explore the universe and discover its truths.*

R3: *They wished to serve, and they did.*

All: *They served all of us.*

R3: *We've grown used to wonders in this century. It's hard to dazzle us. But for twenty-five years, the United States space program has been doing just that. We've grown used to the idea of space, and, perhaps we forget that we've only just begun. We're still pioneers. They, the members of the* Challenger *crew, were pioneers.*

R4: *And I want to say something to the school children of America who were watching the live coverage of the shuttle's takeoff. I know it's hard to understand, but sometimes painful things like this happen. It's all part of the process of exploration and discovery. It's all part of taking a chance and expanding man's horizons. The future doesn't belong to the fainthearted; it belongs to the brave. The* Challenger *crew was pulling us into the future, and we'll continue to follow them.*

R1: *I've always had great faith in and respect for our space program. And what happened today does nothing to diminish it. We don't hide our space program. We don't keep secrets and cover things up. We do it all up front and in public. That's the way freedom is, and we wouldn't change it for a minute.*

All: *We'll continue our quest in space.*

The Space Shuttle *Challenger*: A Speech Delivered by Ronald Reagan *(cont.)*

R2: *There will be more shuttle flights and more shuttle crews*

R3: *and, yes, more volunteers,*

R4: *more civilians, and more teachers in space.*

All: **Nothing ends here; our hopes and our journeys continue.**

R1: *I want to add that I wish I could talk to every man and woman who works for NASA, or who worked on this mission and tell them: "Your dedication and professionalism have moved and impressed us for decades. And we know of your anguish. We share it."*

R2: *There's a coincidence today. On this day three hundred and ninety years ago, the great explorer Sir Francis Drake died aboard ship off the coast of Panama. In his lifetime, the great frontiers were the oceans, and a historian later said,*

R3: *"He lived by the sea, died on it, and was buried in it."*

R4: *Well, today, we can say of the* Challenger *crew: Their dedication was, like Drake's, complete.*

R1: *The crew of the space shuttle* Challenger *honored us by the manner in which they lived their lives.*

R2: *We will never forget them, nor the last time we saw them, this morning, as they prepared for their journey and waved goodbye and "slipped the surly bonds of earth" to "touch the face of God."*

Background Information

The Space Shuttle *Challenger* had flown nine missions before the tragedy that occurred on January 28, 1986. This special mission was the first of its kind to take a teacher into space. Christa McAuliffe is still honored today for her bravery in joining this mission.

#50113—Building Fluency through Practice and Performance © *Shell Education*

An Interview with Six American First Ladies

Written and Arranged by Stephen Griffith
A reader's theater for seven voices

Interviewer: I'm *[insert name here]* with WUSA History Radio and today we're talking about, and to, first ladies of the land. The wives of American presidents. In our studio today we are fortunate to have Jacqueline Kennedy, wife of the 35th president of the United States, John F. Kennedy; Claudia "Lady Bird" Johnson, wife of the 36th president, Lyndon Baines Johnson; Rosalynn Carter, wife of the 39th president, Jimmy Carter; Nancy Reagan, wife of the 40th president, Ronald Reagan; Barbara Bush, wife of George Herbert Walker Bush, the 41st president; and Hillary Rodham Clinton, wife of Bill Clinton, the 42nd president of the United States.

Thank you, ladies, for being here today. Abigail Adams, the wife of the second president, John Adams, said *"No man ever prospered in the world without the consent and cooperation of his wife."* I think the women in this room are proof of what Mrs. Adams said.

My first question is: What is it like to be first lady? I know Betty Ford, who couldn't be here today, said it was *"like being thrown into a river without knowing how to swim."*

Nancy Reagan: Yes, I don't think anybody can ever imagine how much of a change it is until you're actually here. Nobody can ever prepare you for the scrutiny that you're under. You live a magnified life, which means the highs are higher, the lows are lower, with every move you make exaggerated by the tremendous scrutiny of the media. It's a high-wire existence, and I wouldn't trade the experience for even extra years added to my life.

Interviewer: Thank you Mrs. Reagan.

Jacqueline Kennedy: *"The one thing I did not want to be called is first lady. It sounded like a saddle horse. I wanted to be known simply as Mrs. Kennedy and not as the first lady."*

Claudia Johnson: *"The first lady is, and always has been, an unpaid public servant elected by one person, her husband."*

An Interview with Six American First Ladies *(cont.)*

Barbara Bush: *"It's the darndest thing, and I think the ladies will agree, that the day before you are married to the president-elect nobody cares what you say, and the day after he is the president-elect people think you are brilliant and your causes are very good."*

Interviewer: What is the role of the first lady and what influence does she have?

Nancy Reagan: *"The primary role of a first lady is to look after a president's health and well being. And if that interferes with other plans, so be it. No first lady needs to make apologies for looking out for her husband's personal welfare . . . the first lady is, first of all, a wife.*

"As for influence, for eight years I lived with the president. If that doesn't give you special access, I don't know what does. If the president has a bully pulpit, then the first lady has a white glove pulpit. It is more refined, perhaps, more restricted, more ceremonial, but it's a bully pulpit all the same."

Rosalynn Carter: *"I don't think that there is any doubt that the first ladies have some influence on their husbands, because they are close to them, they talk with them all the time. They have the president's ear. I don't think there is any doubt about it."*

Interviewer: Tell me about the White House, your official "home."

Jacqueline Kennedy: *"The Oval Room is my favorite room in the White House—the one where I think the heart of the White House is—where the president receives all the heads of state who visit him—where the honor guard is formed to march downstairs to 'Hail to the Chief'—All ceremonies and all the private talks that really matter happen in that room—and it has the most beautiful proportions of any in the White House."*

Hillary Rodham Clinton: *"We love the second floor of the White House. We are left totally alone. We don't have the Secret Service people following us and we can tell the staff we will take care of ourselves, so it's like being in your own house when you are up there. We've actually had more family time together because, as I've told my friends, the president kind of lives above the store, and we manage to have dinner together practically every night."*

#50113—Building Fluency through Practice and Performance

An Interview with Six American First Ladies *(cont.)*

Interviewer: Are there any final thoughts about being first lady that you would like to share with listeners?

Hillary Rodham Clinton: *"Yes. The American people have made the role of the first lady one of the most important jobs in the country. It happened because each first lady from Martha Washington onward contributed to her husband's historical reputation. It is a tribute to American women that, coming from different social and economic backgrounds, from many different geographical regions, and with diverse educational preparation, each first lady served our country so well. Each left her own mark, and each teaches us something special about our history."*

Claudia Johnson: *"As first lady, you come to know your country more, in depth, in a rare and wonderful way. And you wind up more in love with it than you ever were."*

Rosalynn Carter: *"I would advise any young person to go into politics. We're always looking for candidates that have new approaches to problems. It is hard, not easy. But we need good people in politics so bad."*

Barbara Bush: *"Somewhere out in this audience may even be someone who will one day follow my footsteps, and preside over the White House as the president's spouse. I wish him well!"*

All: [Laugh]

Interviewer: Thank you all for sharing with us some of your thoughts about being a part of the history of this great country.

Background Information

This reader's theater is based on actual quotations by the first ladies. A lot is expected of modern first ladies. Their job is far more complex than the first ladies of the early presidents. Women are more respected in society, so today's first ladies receive more opportunities to make change.

September 11, 2001

Author unknown, Arranged and revised by Lorraine Griffith
A piece for two voices

R1: On Monday, it was September 10, 2001.

R2: On Tuesday, it was September 11th.

R1: On Monday, we emailed jokes.

R2: On Tuesday, we did not.

R1: On Monday, we thought that we were secure.

R2: On Tuesday, we learned better.

R1: On Monday, we were talking about athletes as heroes.

R2: On Tuesday, we learned our real heroes lived in fire stations and police stations.

R1: On Monday, we were irritated that our rebate checks had not arrived.

R2: On Tuesday, we gave money away to people we had never met.

R1: On Monday, people argued with their kids about picking up their rooms.

R2: On Tuesday, the same people could not get home fast enough to hug their kids.

R1: On Monday, people were upset that they had to wait six minutes for a burger and fries at a drive-through.

R2: On Tuesday, people didn't care about waiting six hours at the Red Cross to give blood for the dying.

R1: On Monday, we waved flags signifying our cultural diversity.

R2: On Tuesday, we waved only the American flag.

R1: On Monday, there were people trying to separate each other by race, sex, color and creed.

R2: On Tuesday, we were all holding hands.

September 11, 2001 *(cont.)*

R1: On Monday, we were men or women, black or white, old or young, rich or poor.

R2: On Tuesday, we were Americans.

R1: On Monday, politicians argued about budget surpluses.

R2: On Tuesday, grief stricken, they sang "God Bless America."

R1: On Monday, we had families.

R2: On Tuesday, we had orphans.

R1: On Monday, people went to work as usual.

R2: On Tuesday, they died.

R1: On Monday, it was September 10, 2001.

R2: On Tuesday, it was September 11th.

Background Information

On September 11, 2001, four planes crashed in the United States. Two planes crashed into the World Trade Center Twin Towers in New York City. One plane crashed into the Pentagon outside Washington, D.C. A final plane went down in a field in Pennsylvania. Firefighters and police officers rushed to the scenes to save people. Almost 3,000 men, women, and children died that day.

Performance Suggestion

Read this with a partner. Ask members of your family about their memories of that terrible day in American history. Use the emotions and feelings that are shared with you to find the right voice for performing this piece. Rehearse your reading and then share this with your class or another class in your school.

America's Songs

George M. Cohan Excerpts

You're a Grand Old Flag

You're a grand old flag,
You're a high-flying flag
And forever in peace may you wave.
You're the emblem of the land I love.
The home of the free and the brave.

Ev'ry heart beats true
'neath the Red, White and Blue,
Where there's never a boast or brag.
Should old acquaintances be forgot,
Keep your eye on the grand old flag.

Yankee Doodle Dandy

I'm a Yankee Doodle Dandy,
A Yankee Doodle, do or die;
A real live nephew of my Uncle Sam,
Born on the Fourth of July.

I've got a Yankee Doodle sweetheart,
She's my Yankee Doodle joy.
Yankee Doodle came to London,
Just to ride the ponies;
I am the Yankee Doodle Boy.

George M. Cohan Excerpts *(cont.)*

Over There

Over there, over there,
Send the word, send the word over there—
That the Yanks are coming,
The Yanks are coming,
The drums rum-tumming Ev'rywhere.
So prepare, say a pray'r,
Send the word, send the word to beware.
We'll be over, we're coming over,
And we won't come back till it's over
Over there.

Background Information

George M. Cohan was an American composer, lyricist, actor, singer, dancer, director, and producer of theatrical shows. He was known as the "man who owned Broadway" in the early twentieth century. He is considered the father of American musical comedy. He wrote many patriotic songs, including these three songs.

Dixie

By Daniel Decatur Emmett

I wish I was in the land of cotton,
Old times there are not forgotten,
Look away, Look away, Look away, Dixie land!
In Dixie land where I was born in, early on one frosty mornin',
Look away, Look away, Look away, Dixie land.

Chorus
Then I wish I was in Dixie, Hooray! Hooray!
In Dixie land I'll take my stand, to live and die in Dixie,
Away, away, away down south in Dixie,
Away, away, away down south in Dixie.

Background Information

This song was written by Daniel Decatur Emmett of Mount Vernon, Ohio. It was first heard in September 1859 in New York. However, "Dixie" is best known as the anthem of the Confederacy during the American Civil War. It was also the favorite song of Abraham Lincoln and was played at his inauguration. Daniel Emmett was ostracized in the North for writing a song associated with the South.

The Battle Cry of Freedom

By George F. Root

Yes, we'll rally round the flag, boys, we'll rally once again,
Shouting the battle cry of Freedom;
We will rally from the hillside, we'll gather from the plain,
Shouting the battle cry of Freedom!

Chorus
The Union forever! Hurrah, boys, Hurrah!
Down with the traitors, up with the stars;
While we rally round the flag, boys, rally once again,
Shouting the battle cry of freedom!

We are springing to the call of our brothers gone before,
Shouting the battle cry of Freedom;
And we'll fill our vacant ranks with a million free men more,
Shouting the battle cry of Freedom!

Chorus

We will welcome to our numbers the loyal, true and brave,
Shouting the battle cry of Freedom;
And although they may be poor, not a man shall be a slave,
Shouting the battle cry of Freedom!

Chorus

So we're springing to the call from the East and from the West,
Shouting the battle cry of Freedom;
And we'll hurl the rebel crew from the land we love best,
Shouting the battle cry of Freedom!

Chorus

Background Information

Written in 1862 by George Root, this song was the most effective rallying song of the North. Soldiers sang it in battle, in camps and on the long march. The naturalness and spontaneity in the melody and rhythm give it those national qualities of a patriotic song. Abraham Lincoln used it as a campaign song in the presidential election of 1864.

#50113—Building Fluency through Practice and Performance

Brother, Can You Spare a Dime?

By E. Y. Harburg and J. Gorney

They used to tell me I was building a dream
And so I followed the mob
When there was earth to plow or guns to bear
I was always there, right on the job.

They used to tell me I was building a dream
With peace and glory ahead
Why should I be standing in line
Just waiting for bread?

Once I built a railroad, made it run,
Made it race against time.
Once I built a railroad,
Now it's done.
Brother, can you spare a dime?

Once I built a tower to the sun,
Brick and rivet and lime.
Once I built a tower—now it's done.
Brother, can you spare a dime?

Once in khaki suits,
Gee, we looked swell,
Full of that Yankee-Doodle-de-dom.
Half a million boots went slogging through Hell,
I was the kid with the drum.

Say, don't you remember? They called me Al,
It was Al all the time.
Say, don't you remember? I'm your pal!
Buddy, can you spare a dime?

Background Information

This song was a popular tune during the Great Depression. It reflected the struggle and desperation that Americans felt as the national economy failed and people lost their jobs, homes, farms, and pride.

Happy Days Are Here Again

By Jack Yellen and Milton Alger

Happy days are here again!
The skies above are clear again.
Let us sing a song of cheer again
Happy days are here again!

All together, shout it now!
There's no one who can doubt it now,
So let's tell the world about it now
Happy days are here again!

Your cares and troubles are gone—
There'll be no more from now on!
Happy days are here again,
The skies above are clear again;
Let us sing a song of cheer again—
Happy days are here again!

Background Information

This song was a campaign song for Franklin D. Roosevelt. It reflected the optimistic attitude that Roosevelt wished to impart on the American people who had suffered much through the Great Depression.

#50113—Building Fluency through Practice and Performance

How the Workers Can Be Free

By William Foster

Shall song and music be forgot
When workingmen combine?
With love united may they not
Have power almost divine?
Shall idle drones still live like kings
On labor not their own?
Shall true men starve, while thieves and rings
Reap where they have not sown?
No! by our cause eternal, No!
It shall not forever be;
And Union men will ere long show
How the workers can be free.
No! by our cause eternal, No!
It shall not forever be;
And Union men will ere long show
How the workers can be free.

Background Information

This song was taken from the "ode card" of the American Federation of Labor. It is to be sung to the tune "Auld Lang Syne."

Military Service Songs

These are songs that are commonly associated with the military branches of the United States.

Army

Over hill, over dale
As we hit the dusty trail,
And those caissons go rolling along.
In and out, hear them shout,
Counter march and right about,
And those caissons go rolling along.

Chorus
Then it's hi! hi! hee!
In the field artillery,
Shout out your numbers loud and strong,
For where e'er you go,
You will always know
That those caissons go rolling along.

In the storm, in the night,
Action left or action right
See those caissons go rolling along
Limber front, limber rear,
Prepare to mount your cannoneer
And those caissons go rolling along.

Chorus

#50113—Building Fluency through Practice and Performance

© *Shell Education*

Military Service Songs *(cont.)*

Navy

Anchors Aweigh, my boys, Anchors Aweigh.
Farewell to college joys, we sail at break of day-ay-ay-ay.
Through our last night on shore, drink to the foam,
Until we meet once more,
Here's wishing you a happy voyage home.

Marine Corps

From the Halls of Montezuma
To the Shores of Tripoli
We fight our country's battles
In the air, on land and sea.
First to fight for right and freedom
And to keep our honor clean;
We are proud to claim the title
of United States Marine.

Our flag's unfurled to every breeze
From dawn to setting sun;
We have fought in every clime and place
Where we could take a gun.
In the snow of far-off Northern lands
And in sunny tropic scenes;
You will find us always on the job—
The United States Marines.

Military Service Songs *(cont.)*

Air Force

Off we go into the wild blue yonder,
Climbing high into the sun.
Here they come, zooming to meet our thunder;
At 'em boys, give 'er the gun!
Down we dive, spouting our flame from under,
Off with one helluva roar!
We live in fame or go down in flame. Hey!
Nothing'll stop the U.S. Air Force!

Coast Guard

We're always ready for the call,
We place our trust in Thee.
Through howling gale and shot and shell,
To win our victory.
"Semper Paratus" is our guide,
Our pledge, our motto, too.
We're "Always Ready," do or die!
Aye! Coast Guard, we fight for you.

Correlation to American History

Contents of the Teacher Resource CD

The CD has a *Microsoft Word*™ file and an Adobe PDF for each text. The PDF can be used to project the texts for large-group use or to print copies of the texts for the students. The *Word* files are useful for teachers who want to change the texts or lower the reading levels of the texts.

Page	Title	Filenames
12	I Hear America Singing	amrcasng.doc amrcasng.pdf
13	From the Mouths and Pens of the American Presidents	presdent.doc presdent.pdf
24	November: A Time of Thanks and Remembrance in America in Poetry, Song, and Speech	november.doc november.pdf
29	Patriots, Tories, and Neutrals: Revolutionary Opinions	patriots.doc patriots.pdf
31	The Declaration of the Independence	dclrtion.doc dclrtion.pdf
36	E PLURIBUS UNUM	pluribus.doc pluribus.pdf
38	Preamble to the Constitution	preamble.doc preamble.pdf
43	Francis Scott Key's "The Star-Spangled Banner"	spangled.doc spangled.pdf
48	My Name Is Old Glory	oldglory.doc oldglory.pdf
52	The Statue of Liberty	liberty.doc liberty.pdf
55	Emma Lazarus and "The New Colossus"	colossus.doc colossus.pdf
58	Events in the History of James W.C. Pennington: Formerly a Slave	penigton.doc penigton.pdf
62	The Underground Railcar	undrgrnd.doc undrgrnd.pdf
64	Company Aytch (H)	company.doc company.pdf
65	Voices from the Civil War	civilwar.doc civilwar.pdf
81	Gettysburg and Mr. Lincoln's Speech	lincoln.doc lincoln.pdf
87	Carl Sandburg on World War I	sandburg.doc sandburg.pdf
89	Voices from The Great Depression	deprsion.doc deprsion.pdf
94	Duty, Honor, Country: Excerpts from Douglas MacArthur's Farewell to West Point, May 1962	macarthr.doc macarthr.pdf
97	Remember the Ladies	ladies.doc ladies.pdf
99	A Declaration of Sentiments	sentimnt.doc sentimnt.pdf
102	Excerpts from the Emancipation Proclamation	prclmtin.doc prclmtin.pdf

Page	Title	Filenames
104	Emancipation	emancptn.doc emancptn.pdf
106	It Makes My Heart Sick: Chief Joseph Speaks	joseph.doc joseph.pdf
113	I Do Not Believe in Woman Suffrage: Based on the Writings of Marie Jenney Howe, 1913	suffrage.doc suffrage.pdf
116	From Adversity to Success: The Jesse Owens Story	jesseown.doc jesseown.pdf
122	Rosa Parks, December 1, 1955	rosapark.doc rosapark.pdf
126	Excerpts from President John F. Kennedy's Civil Rights Address, June 13, 1963	kennedy.doc kennedy.pdf
131	Voices from the Civil Rights Movement	cvlrghts.doc cvlrghts.pdf
132	A Tribute To Dr. Martin Luther King Jr.	tribute.doc tribute.pdf
135	Excerpts of Remarks by Robert F. Kennedy on the Day of the Assassination of Dr. Martin Luther King Jr.	remarks.doc remarks.pdf
138	The Inauguration of President John Fitzgerald Kennedy	ingrtion.doc ingrtion.pdf
145	The Assassination of John Fitzgerald Kennedy: A Nation Bereaved	asasintn.doc asasintn.pdf
152	Landing on the Moon	landmoon.doc landmoon.pdf
156	The Space Shuttle *Challenger*: A Speech Delivered by Ronald Reagan	chalengr.doc chalengr.pdf
159	An Interview with Six American First Ladies	frstlady.doc frstlady.pdf
162	September 11, 2001	septmber.doc septmber.pdf
165	George M. Cohan Excerpts	cohan.doc cohan.pdf
167	Dixie	dixie.doc dixie.pdf
168	The Battle Cry of Freedom	batlecry.doc batlecry.pdf
169	Brother, Can You Spare a Dime?	dime.doc dime.pdf
170	Happy Days Are Here Again	happy.doc happy.pdf
171	How the Workers Can Be Free	workers.doc workers.pdf
172	Military Service Songs	military.doc military.pdf